MW01110318

WHAT EVERY FAMILY SHOULD KNOW

A
LIFETIME
Record and Organizer

Date

By

From Generation To Generation™

DESIGN AND CONCEPT BY OLEG KAY

Carriage House Communications
Inc.

P.O. Box 2240
Westport, CT 06880

Publishers
Preserving Memories From Generation To Generation

Other Titles
by
Carriage House Communications, Inc.

School Years/Childhood Memories

My Family Tree
Wall Hanging

Christmas Memories

My Family Heritage

Grandmother's Family Heritage

My Irish Heritage

Origin of Irish Families
Wall Hanging

Treasured Recipes
Organizer of Edible Nostalgia

Classic Blank Books
Fine Editions

ISBN 0-89786-098-5

Table of Contents

CAUTION

In reference to wills—Chapter Two • VITAL PAPERS—laws and regulations vary on the same issue from state to state—the same issue is subject to different interpretations. It is important that you seek advise about your state's current laws and how they apply to your personal circumstance.

Legal forms do not always meet all your needs. The "SAMPLE FORMAT" legal forms in this book is to give you an overview and to inform you as to what you need to know—a starting point for you to make right decisions to meet all your needs.

There is no substitute for common sense. On important legal matters when it involves large sums of money, real property and personal assets, it is always advisable to consult with a competent attorney.

Family & the Need to Know

*T*his book is for you and for the people that you care about. The best decisions for today and tomorrow can only be made based on vital facts. You or your family must have all the vital facts in front of you in order to evaluate your options before making the right decision.

There is no substitute for common sense. By being organized and informed you can avoid costly mistakes and save thousands of dollars in fees. For your own peace of mind it is always best to know all your options today in order to make the important decisions for tomorrow.

Illnesses are an unfortunate yet unavoidable feature of life. Your and your family's medical records are as important as property deeds, birth and marriage records because many illnesses are genetically related. The more information you have the more you can conclude what your or someone's risk is inheriting a disease.

Because most of us do not make regular use of our important documents, we may forget where they are or the fact that they exist. Most documents are simply scattered about the house. Do not take your vital documents for granted. Know what you have and where it is!

Most of us have had the experience of needing certain vital papers and information and not being able to find them. It is a costly and frustrating experience. Chances are that no one but you knows where all your vital papers are. The probable truth is that even you would have trouble finding essential documents in an unexpected crisis. What if you became seriously ill or temporarily incapacitated? Would your family or close relatives know where to find your insurance policies, forms and information to take care of your financial affairs? Is your family familiar with the details of your financial situation? Can they handle your estate in your and

their best interests? Do they know where you keep your vital papers and important documents? Do you have a will? For most people the answer to one or more of these questions is "No," which means that you are disorganized and your family is more unprotected than you care to admit.

This book is designed to help you give those you care about a complete peace of mind. It is a foolproof way to impart a knowledge of your financial situation that will enable you and others to make intelligent plans for the future.

In the process of compiling the necessary data, you also will be making order of your present holdings—something that many of us neglect. This order—the itemization of possessions, assets, and liabilities—is also the first step in drawing up a will. Creating and maintaining such an inventory is essential in evaluating your estate and determining its distribution. And these decisions must be made. It took Picasso's heirs seven costly and bitter years to settle his estate; and not because of the countless millions in it, but simply because he refused to prepare a will.

This book is also the best way to keep a continuing account of your property in one convenient place. You should review it periodically, adding new items as they come in, deleting those that have been disposed of or sold, and recording new ideas or intentions. Keep the book in a safe place, and one to which your family has access. This is an invaluable guide for today and tomorrow.

Remember: A will, a Living Will and a Living Trust are the most important documents. When this book is completed it will contain all the necessary information and contents of your estate. Consult a competent attorney with regard to a proper will. There should be no excuse not to have a will.

A carefully prepared record of your family is of great importance. This record should contain all of the benchmark activities of each member of the family. In preparing the record, care should be taken to provide as much information as possible—for example, the town and state where each family member was born; the date of birth, state, and town where each died; the cause of death; and the town, date, and state where each married.

If you do not preserve what you know, later generations will be deprived of crucial information. The passage of time depletes the storehouse of available information that only you possess.

As powerful as a key experience may be at the time, memories fade with the passing years. Trying to recall the details of an important event one or more decades earlier can be an exercise in frustration. Jotting down these important facts as they happen is a way of assuring they are not lost forever.

The importance of such recorded information, moreover, can have significance far beyond that of simply filling generational gaps in a family's continuum. Carefully documented events can provide evidence critical in determining family related litigation. In allocating the proceeds of a divorce, for example, or even more complex—the proceeds of a separation following the death of one of the parties, the ability to document what happened when can be paramount in determining the quality of life of the parties involved.

Similarly, painstakingly recorded medical information—including prescribed medication and the dates and nature of specific illnesses—can aid in determining diagnoses of diseases that may transcend generations. Fewer than half the states permit patients to see their medical records on demand, and even in these states there may be restrictions. This being so, it is extremely important that you take matters into your own hands and keep good records yourself—for your entire family.

For all of these reasons, the key in using this volume is thoroughness. Whatever facts or memories you set down on these pages will be of value in the situations described above only if they are recorded in enough detail—and with enough documentation—to be definitive.

But no matter how the information you record here is used, it all becomes a point of departure for your descendants. You are the link between the past and the future. There is no better gift to your descendants than the priceless record of their heritage.

WHERE TO WRITE FOR BIRTH, MARRIAGE AND DEATH RECORDS.
The state and county offices which keep these records have official titles which vary from state to state. To help you contact the proper office the Department of Public Health Services has printed three booklets: 1) Where to Write for Birth and Death Records. DHEW Publication No. PHS 76-1142. 2) Where to Write for Marriage Records. DHEW Publication No. PHS 76-1144. 3) Where to Write for Divorce Records. DHEW Publication No. PHS 76-1145. These booklets are available for a minimal fee from any government printing office or a GPO Bookstore, or you may simply write to:

Superintendent of Documents
U.S. Government Printing Office
Washington, DC 20402

For genealogical information on your ancestors write to: Library of the Church of Latter Day Saints, 50 East North Temple Street, Salt Lake City, Utah 84150. No matter where you presently live or what country your ancestors came from this is the best and the largest depository of genealogical records in the world.

Family

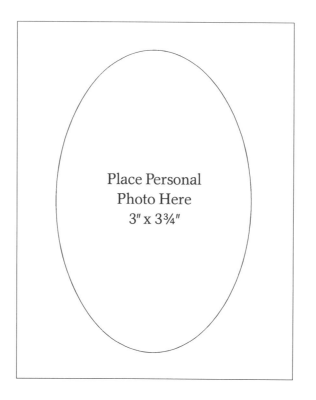

Place Personal
Photo Here
3″ x 3¾″

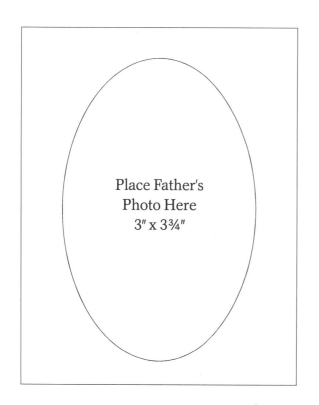

Place Father's
Photo Here
3″ x 3¾″

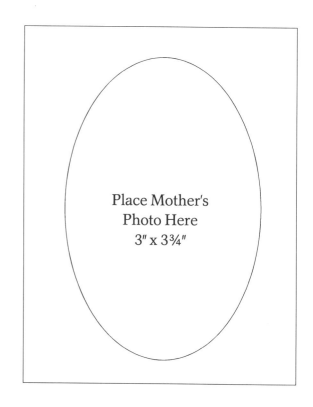

Place Mother's
Photo Here
3″ x 3¾″

Family

YOUR NAME _____
                First   *Middle*   *Last*

Date of Birth _____
          Month   *Day*   *Year*   *Time*

Place of Birth _____
         Street   *City*   *County*   *State or Country*

Birth Certificate Located at: _____ Birth Certificate No. _____

Social Security No. _____ Occupations _____

Health _____

Your FATHER'S FULL NAME _____

Place of Birth _____ Birth Date _____
         Street   *City*   *County*   *State or Country*

Birth Certificate Located at: _____ Birth Certificate No. _____

Social Security No. _____ Occupations _____

Health _____ Cause of Death _____
                                         Date

His Brothers and Sisters _____

His Father's Full Name _____ Birth Date _____

Occupations _____

Health _____ Cause of Death _____
                                         Date

His Mother's Full Name _____ Birth Date _____

Health _____ Cause of Death _____
                                         Date

Your MOTHER'S FULL NAME _____

Place of Birth _____ Birth Date _____
         Street   *City*   *County*   *State or Country*

Birth Certificate Located at: _____ Birth Certificate No. _____

Social Security No. _____ Occupations _____

Health _____ Cause of Death _____
                                         Date

Her Brothers and Sisters _____

Her Father's Full Name _____ Birth Date _____

Occupations _____

Health _____ Cause of Death _____
                                         Date

Her Mother's Full Name _____ Birth Date _____

Health _____ Cause of Death _____
                                         Date

9

My Brothers & Sisters

NAME_____
First   Middle   Last

Date of Birth_____
Month   Day   Year   Time

Place of Birth_____
Street or Hospital City County State or Country

Health_____ Occupations _____

Cause of Death_____ Date _____

Spouse_____
First Name   Middle   Last

Children_____

NAME_____
First   Middle   Last

Date of Birth_____
Month   Day   Year   Time

Place of Birth_____
Street or Hospital City County State or Country

Health_____ Occupations _____

Cause of Death_____ Date _____

Spouse_____
First Name   Middle   Last

Children_____

NAME_____
First   Middle   Last

Date of Birth_____
Month   Day   Year   Time

Place of Birth_____
Street or Hospital City County State or Country

Health_____ Occupations _____

Cause of Death_____ Date _____

Spouse_____
First Name   Middle   Last

Children_____

NAME_____
First   Middle   Last

Date of Birth_____
Month   Day   Year   Time

Place of Birth_____
Street or Hospital City County State or Country

Health_____ Occupations _____

Cause of Death_____ Date _____

Spouse_____
First Name   Middle   Last

Children_____

My Brothers & Sisters

NAME_____
         First   *Middle*   *Last*

Date of Birth_____
       Month   *Day*   *Year*   *Time*

Place of Birth_____
    Street or Hospital   *City*   *County*   *State or Country*

Health_____ Occupations_____

Cause of Death_____ Date _____

Spouse_____
    First Name   *Middle*   *Last*

Children_____

NAME_____
    First   *Middle*   *Last*

Date of Birth_____
   Month *Day* *Year* *Time*

Place of Birth_____
  Street or Hospital *City* *County* *State or Country*

Health_____ Occupations_____

Cause of Death_____ Date _____

Spouse_____
  First Name *Middle* *Last*

Children_____

NAME_____
  First *Middle* *Last*

Date of Birth_____
  Month *Day* *Year* *Time*

Place of Birth_____
  Street or Hospital *City* *County* *State or Country*

Health_____ Occupations_____

Cause of Death_____ Date _____

Spouse_____
  First Name *Middle* *Last*

Children_____

NAME_____
  First *Middle* *Last*

Date of Birth_____
  Month *Day* *Year* *Time*

Place of Birth_____
  Street or Hospital *City* *County* *State or Country*

Health_____ Occupations_____

Cause of Death_____ Date _____

Spouse_____
  First Name *Middle* *Last*

Children_____

My Father's Parents

My Grandfather

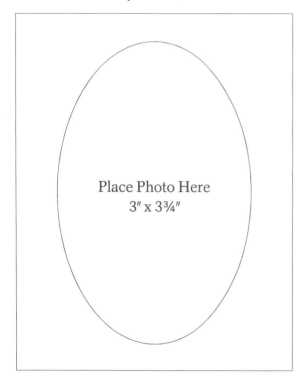

Place Photo Here
3" x 3¾"

Paternal

Full Name _____

Birth Date _____

Place of Birth: City _____ State _____

Country _____

_____

Occupations _____

_____

_____

Health _____

Cause of Death _____
                                    Date

Brothers and Sisters _____

_____

_____

_____

_____

Date of Photograph _____

My Grandmother

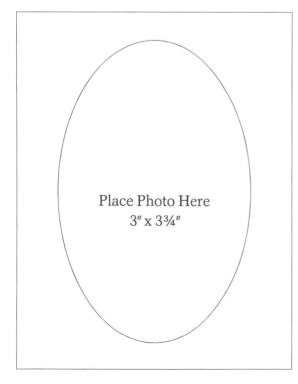

Place Photo Here
3" x 3¾"

Paternal

Full Name _____

Birth Date _____

Place of Birth: City _____ State _____

Country _____

_____

Occupations _____

_____

_____

Health _____

Cause of Death _____
                                    Date

Brothers and Sisters _____

_____

_____

_____

Date of Photograph _____

Father's Brothers & Sisters

NAME_____

First   Middle   Last

Date of Birth_____

Month   Day   Year   Time

Place of Birth_____

Street or Hospital   City   County   State or Country

Health_____ Occupations_____

Cause of Death_____ Date_____

Spouse_____

First Name   Middle   Last

Children_____

NAME_____

First   Middle   Last

Date of Birth_____

Month   Day   Year   Time

Place of Birth_____

Street or Hospital   City   County   State or Country

Health_____ Occupations_____

Cause of Death_____ Date_____

Spouse_____

First Name   Middle   Last

Children_____

NAME_____

First   Middle   Last

Date of Birth_____

Month   Day   Year   Time

Place of Birth_____

Street or Hospital   City   County   State or Country

Health_____ Occupations_____

Cause of Death_____ Date_____

Spouse_____

First Name   Middle   Last

Children_____

NAME_____

First   Middle   Last

Date of Birth_____

Month   Day   Year   Time

Place of Birth_____

Street or Hospital   City   County   State or Country

Health_____ Occupations_____

Cause of Death_____ Date_____

Spouse_____

First Name   Middle   Last

Children_____

Father's Brothers & Sisters

NAME_____
        First   Middle   Last

Date of Birth_____
        Month   Day   Year   Time

Place of Birth_____
        Street or Hospital   City   County   State or Country

Health_____ Occupations_____

Cause of Death_____ Date_____

Spouse_____
        First Name   Middle   Last

Children_____

NAME_____
        First   Middle   Last

Date of Birth_____
        Month   Day   Year   Time

Place of Birth_____
        Street or Hospital   City   County   State or Country

Health_____ Occupations_____

Cause of Death_____ Date_____

Spouse_____
        First Name   Middle   Last

Children_____

NAME_____
        First   Middle   Last

Date of Birth_____
        Month   Day   Year   Time

Place of Birth_____
        Street or Hospital   City   County   State or Country

Health_____ Occupations_____

Cause of Death_____ Date_____

Spouse_____
        First Name   Middle   Last

Children_____

NAME_____
        First   Middle   Last

Date of Birth_____
        Month   Day   Year   Time

Place of Birth_____
        Street or Hospital   City   County   State or Country

Health_____ Occupations_____

Cause of Death_____ Date_____

Spouse_____
        First Name   Middle   Last

Children_____

My Great Grandfather

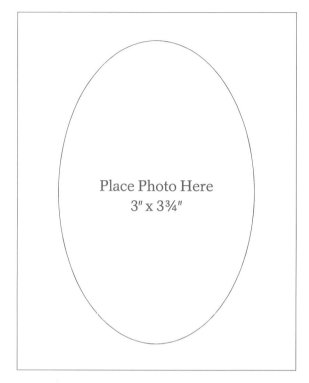

Place Photo Here
3" x 3¾"

My Great Grandmother

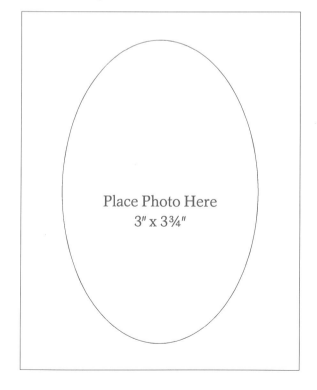

Place Photo Here
3" x 3¾"

Maternal

Full Name _____

Birth Date _____

Place of Birth: City _____ State _____

Country _____

_____

Occupations _____

_____

_____

Health _____

Cause of Death _____
                                            Date

Brothers and Sisters _____

_____

_____

_____

_____

Date of Photograph _____

Maternal

Full Name _____

Birth Date _____

Place of Birth: City _____ State _____

Country _____

_____

Occupations _____

_____

_____

Health _____

Cause of Death _____
                                            Date

Brothers and Sisters _____

_____

_____

_____

_____

Date of Photograph _____

My Father's Grandparents

My Great Grandfather

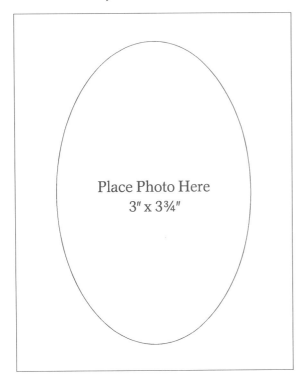

Place Photo Here
3" x 3¾"

Paternal

Full Name _____

Birth Date _____

Place of Birth: City _____ State _____

Country _____

_____

Occupations _____

_____

_____

Health _____

Cause of Death _____
                                    Date

Brothers and Sisters _____

_____

_____

_____

_____

Date of Photograph _____

My Great Grandmother

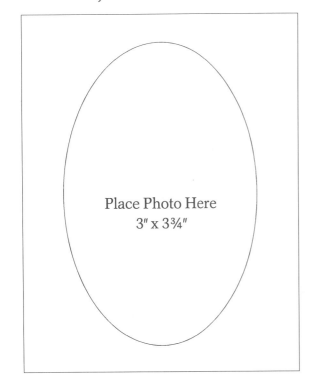

Place Photo Here
3" x 3¾"

Paternal

Full Name _____

Birth Date _____

Place of Birth: City _____ State _____

Country _____

_____

Occupations _____

_____

_____

Health _____

Cause of Death _____
                                    Date

Brothers and Sisters _____

_____

_____

_____

_____

Date of Photograph _____

Father's Medical History

Blood Type _____

General Health _____
_____

Inherited illnesses _____
_____

Birthmarks or scars _____
_____

Severe illnesses, allergies, and injuries _____
_____
_____
_____

Did he drink? _____ Did he smoke? _____

Did he suffer from depression? _____
_____
_____

When did he die?   Month _____ Day _____ Year _____

Cause of Death _____

Place of Burial: City/Town _____ State/Country _____
_____

Anecdotes _____
_____
_____
_____
_____
_____
_____
_____
_____
_____
_____

Mother's Family

Place Your Mother's
Photo Here
3" x 3¾"

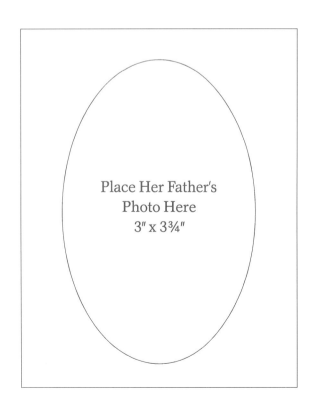

Place Her Father's
Photo Here
3" x 3¾"

Place Her Mother's
Photo Here
3" x 3¾"

Your MOTHER'S FULL MAIDEN NAME _____
  First Middle Last

Date of Birth _____
  Month Day Year Time

Place of Birth _____

_____
  Street City County State or Country

Birth Certificate Located at: _____ *Birth Certificate No.* _____

Social Security No. _____ *Occupations* _____

Health _____ *Cause of Death* _____
  Date

Her FATHER'S FULL NAME _____

Place of Birth _____ *Birth Date* _____

_____
  Street City County State or Country

Birth Certificate Located at: _____ *Birth Certificate No.* _____

Social Security No. _____ *Occupations* _____

Health _____ *Cause of Death* _____
  Date

His Brothers and Sisters _____

His Father's Full Name _____ *Birth Date* _____

Health _____ *Cause of Death* _____
  Date

His Mother's Full Name _____ *Birth Date* _____

Health _____ *Cause of Death* _____
  Date

Her MOTHER'S FULL NAME _____

Place of Birth _____ *Birth Date* _____

_____
  Street City County State or Country

Birth Certificate Located at: _____ *Birth Certificate No.* _____

Social Security No. _____ *Occupations* _____

Health _____ *Cause of Death* _____
  Date

Her Brothers and Sisters _____

Her Father's Full Name _____ *Birth Date* _____

Health _____ *Cause of Death* _____
  Date

Her Mother's Full Name _____ *Birth Date* _____

Health _____ *Cause of Death* _____
  Date

Mother's Brothers & Sisters

NAME_____
First   Middle   Last

Date of Birth_____
Month   Day   Year   Time

Place of Birth_____
Street or Hospital   City   County   State or Country

Health_____Occupations_____

Cause of Death_____Date_____

Spouse_____
First Name   Middle   Last

Children_____

NAME_____
First   Middle   Last

Date of Birth_____
Month   Day   Year   Time

Place of Birth_____
Street or Hospital   City   County   State or Country

Health_____Occupations_____

Cause of Death_____Date_____

Spouse_____
First Name   Middle   Last

Children_____

NAME_____
First   Middle   Last

Date of Birth_____
Month   Day   Year   Time

Place of Birth_____
Street or Hospital   City   County   State or Country

Health_____Occupations_____

Cause of Death_____Date_____

Spouse_____
First Name   Middle   Last

Children_____

NAME_____
First   Middle   Last

Date of Birth_____
Month   Day   Year   Time

Place of Birth_____
Street or Hospital   City   County   State or Country

Health_____Occupations_____

Cause of Death_____Date_____

Spouse_____
First Name   Middle   Last

Children_____

Mother's Brothers & Sisters

NAME_____
                First   *Middle*   *Last*

Date of Birth_____
          Month   *Day*   *Year*   *Time*

Place of Birth_____
      Street or Hospital   *City*   *County*   *State or Country*

Health_____ Occupations_____

Cause of Death_____ Date_____

Spouse_____
          First Name   *Middle*   *Last*

Children_____

NAME_____
                 First   *Middle*   *Last*

Date of Birth_____
          Month   *Day*   *Year*   *Time*

Place of Birth_____
      Street or Hospital   *City*   *County*   *State or Country*

Health_____ Occupations_____

Cause of Death_____ Date_____

Spouse_____
          First Name   *Middle*   *Last*

Children_____

NAME_____
                 First   *Middle*   *Last*

Date of Birth_____
          Month   *Day*   *Year*   *Time*

Place of Birth_____
      Street or Hospital   *City*   *County*   *State or Country*

Health_____ Occupations_____

Cause of Death_____ Date_____

Spouse_____
          First Name   *Middle*   *Last*

Children_____

NAME_____
                 First   *Middle*   *Last*

Date of Birth_____
          Month   *Day*   *Year*   *Time*

Place of Birth_____
      Street or Hospital   *City*   *County*   *State or Country*

Health_____ Occupations_____

Cause of Death_____ Date_____

Spouse_____
          First Name   *Middle*   *Last*

Children_____

My Mother's Parents

My Grandfather

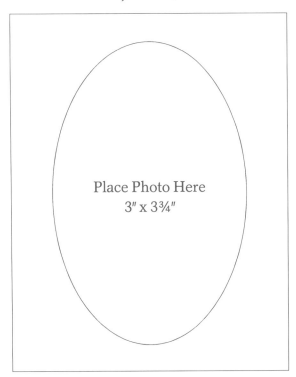

Place Photo Here
3" x 3¾"

Maternal

Full Name _____

Birth Date _____

Place of Birth: City _____ State _____

Country _____

_____

Occupations _____

_____

_____

Health _____

Cause of Death _____
                              Date

Brothers and Sisters _____

_____

_____

_____

_____

Date of Photograph _____

My Grandmother

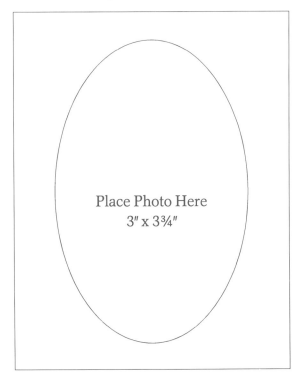

Place Photo Here
3" x 3¾"

Maternal

Full Name _____

Birth Date _____

Place of Birth: City _____ State _____

Country _____

_____

Occupations _____

_____

_____

Health _____

Cause of Death _____
                              Date

Brothers and Sisters _____

_____

_____

_____

_____

Date of Photograph _____

Paternal

My Great Grandfather

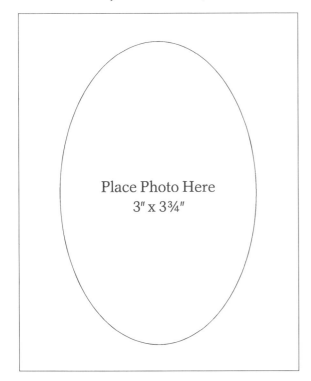

Place Photo Here
3" x 3¾"

Full Name _____

Birth Date _____

Place of Birth: City _____ State _____

Country _____

_____

Occupations _____

_____

_____

Health _____

Cause of Death _____
Date

Brothers and Sisters _____

_____

_____

_____

_____

Date of Photograph _____

Paternal

My Great Grandmother

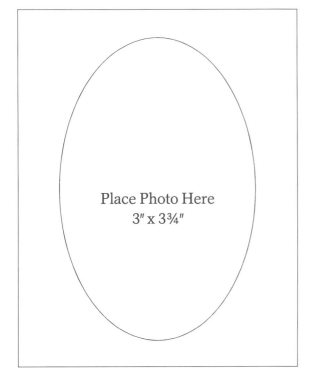

Place Photo Here
3" x 3¾"

Full Name _____

Birth Date _____

Place of Birth: City _____ State _____

Country _____

_____

Occupations _____

_____

_____

Health _____

Cause of Death _____
Date

Brothers and Sisters _____

_____

_____

_____

_____

Date of Photograph _____

Mother's Grandparents

My Great Grandfather

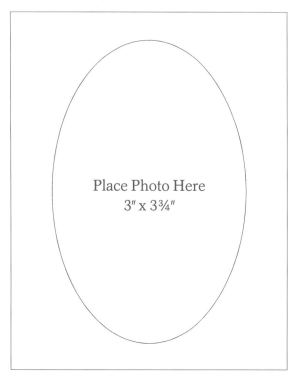

Place Photo Here
3" x 3¾"

Full Name _____

Birth Date _____

Place of Birth: City _____ State _____

Country _____

_____

Occupations _____

_____

_____

Health _____

Cause of Death _____
Date

Brothers and Sisters _____

_____

_____

_____

_____

Date of Photograph _____

My Great Grandmother

Maternal

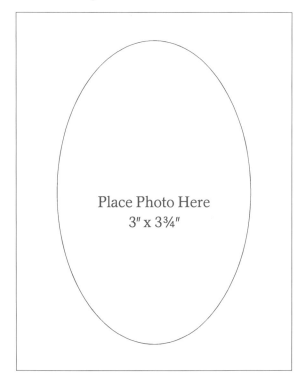

Place Photo Here
3" x 3¾"

Full Name _____

Birth Date _____

Place of Birth: City _____ State _____

Country _____

_____

Occupations _____

_____

_____

Health _____

Cause of Death _____
Date

Brothers and Sisters _____

_____

_____

_____

_____

Date of Photograph _____

24

Mother's Medical History

Blood Type _____

General Health _____

_____

Inherited illnesses _____

_____

Birthmarks or scars _____

_____

Severe illnesses, allergies, and injuries _____

_____

_____

_____

Did she drink? _____ Did she smoke? _____

Did she suffer from depression? _____

_____

_____

When did she die?   Month _____ Day _____ Year _____

Cause of Death _____

Place of Burial: City/Town _____ State/Country _____

_____

Anecdotes _____

_____

_____

_____

_____

_____

_____

_____

_____

_____

_____

_____

_____

Longest Living Relatives

Paternal

Full Name _____ Relation _____
Birth Date _____ Died _____
_____ Lived to be _____
_____
_____

Full Name _____ Relation _____
Birth Date _____ Died _____
_____ Lived to be _____
_____
_____

Full Name _____ Relation _____
Birth Date _____ Died _____
_____ Lived to be _____
_____
_____

Full Name _____ Relation _____
Birth Date _____ Died _____
_____ Lived to be _____
_____
_____

Full Name _____ Relation _____
Birth Date _____ Died _____
_____ Lived to be _____
_____
_____

Full Name _____ Relation _____
Birth Date _____ Died _____
_____ Lived to be _____
_____

Longest Living Relatives

Maternal

Full Name _____ Relation _____
Birth Date _____ Died _____
_____ Lived to be _____
_____
_____

Full Name _____ Relation _____
Birth Date _____ Died _____
_____ Lived to be _____
_____
_____

Full Name _____ Relation _____
Birth Date _____ Died _____
_____ Lived to be _____
_____
_____

Full Name _____ Relation _____
Birth Date _____ Died _____
_____ Lived to be _____
_____
_____

Full Name _____ Relation _____
Birth Date _____ Died _____
_____ Lived to be _____
_____
_____

Full Name _____ Relation _____
Birth Date _____ Died _____
_____ Lived to be _____
_____

My Marriage

Husband's Name _____

Wife's Maiden Name _____

Date and Place of the Ceremony: Month _____ Day _____ Year _____

Town _____ State/Country _____

Who performed the ceremony? _____

Best Man _____

Maid of Honor _____

_____

_____

_____

Your first home after you got married _____

Street _____

City _____ State/Country _____

How long did you live there? _____

_____

_____

_____

_____

Marriage Certificate Located At: _____

_____

_____

Full Name _____

Birth Date _____

City _____ State _____

Hospital _____

Color Eyes _____ Hair _____

_____

Comments _____

_____

_____

_____

_____

Location of Birth Certificate _____

_____

Health _____

_____

_____

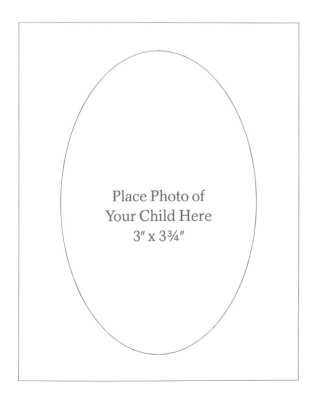

Full Name _____

Birth Date _____

City _____ State _____

Hospital _____

Color Eyes _____ Hair _____

_____

Comments _____

_____

_____

_____

_____

Location of Birth Certificate _____

_____

Health _____

_____

_____

Children

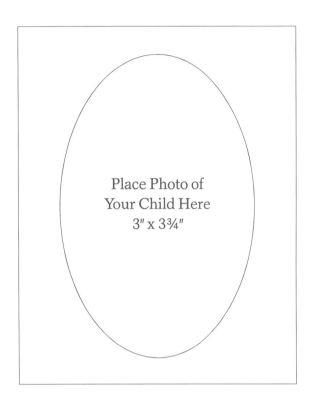

Place Photo of
Your Child Here
3″ x 3¾″

Full Name _____

Birth Date _____

City _____ State _____

Hospital _____

Color Eyes _____ Hair _____

_____

Comments _____

_____

_____

_____

_____

Location of Birth Certificate _____

_____

Health _____

_____

_____

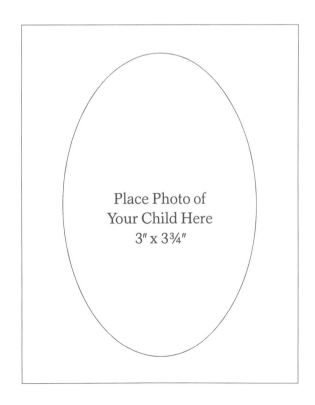

Place Photo of
Your Child Here
3″ x 3¾″

Full Name _____

Birth Date _____

City _____ State _____

Hospital _____

Color Eyes _____ Hair _____

_____

Comments _____

_____

_____

_____

_____

Location of Birth Certificate _____

_____

Health _____

_____

_____

Place Photo of
Your Child Here
3" x 3¾"

Full Name _____

Birth Date _____

City _____ *State* _____

Hospital _____

Color Eyes _____ *Hair* _____

_____

Comments _____

_____

_____

_____

_____

_____

Location of Birth Certificate _____

_____

Health _____

_____

_____

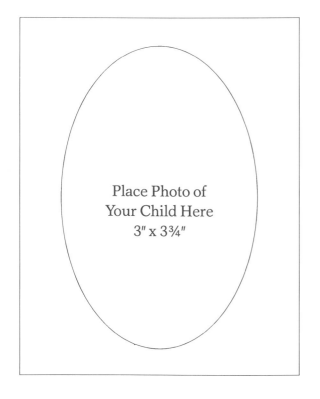

Place Photo of
Your Child Here
3" x 3¾"

Full Name _____

Birth Date _____

City _____ *State* _____

Hospital _____

Color Eyes _____ *Hair* _____

_____

Comments _____

_____

_____

_____

_____

_____

Location of Birth Certificate _____

_____

Health _____

_____

_____

Family Births

Date	Full Name	Relation

Family Births

Date	Full Name	Relation

Grandchildren

Birth Date	Full Name

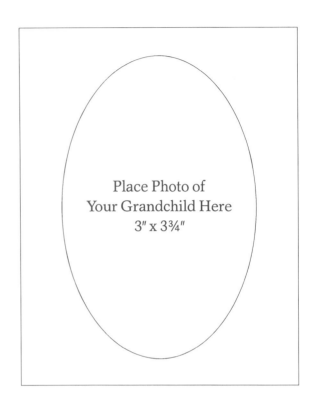

Name _____ *Year* _____

Name _____ *Year* _____

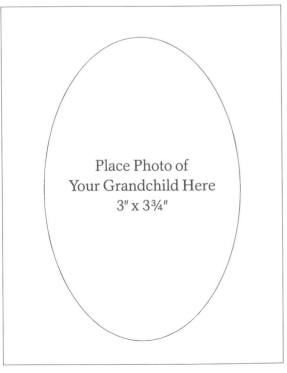

Place Photo of
Your Grandchild Here
3" x 3¾"

Name _____ *Year* _____

Name _____ *Year* _____

Grandchildren

Birth Date	Full Name

Name _____ Year _____

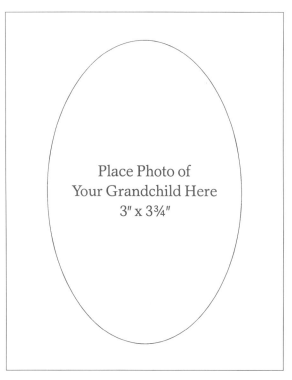

Name _____ Year _____

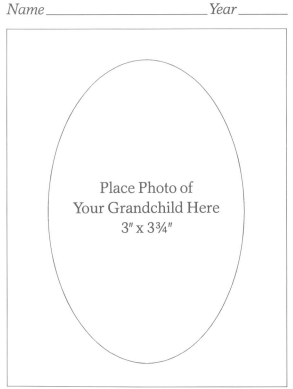

Name _____ Year _____

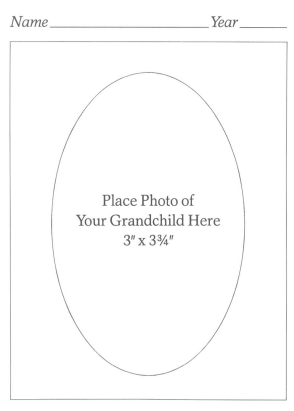

Name _____ Year _____

Family Tree

Father's Family

Father's Full Name-2

Date of Birth

Place of Birth

Date of Marriage

Place of Marriage

Date of Death

Place of Burial

Occupation

Special Interests

Father's Brothers and Sisters

Mother's Brothers and Sisters

My Full Name-1

Date of Birth

Place of Birth

Occupation

Brothers and Sisters

Mother's Family

Mother's Full Name-3

Date of Birth

Place of Birth

Date of Marriage

Place of Marriage

Date of Death

Place of Burial

Occupation

Special Interests

Grandfather's Full Name-4

Date of Birth   Place of Birth

Date of Marriage   Place of Marriage

Date of Death   Place of Burial

Occupation

Special Interests

Great Grandfather's Full Name-8

Date of Birth   Place of Birth

Occupation

Great Grandmother's Full Name-9

Date of Birth   Place of Birth

Special Interests

Grandmother's Full Name-5

Date of Birth   Place of Birth

Date of Marriage   Place of Marriage

Date of Death   Place of Burial

Occupation

Special Interests

Great Grandfather's Full Name-10

Date of Birth   Place of Birth

Occupation

Great Grandmother's Full Name-11

Date of Birth   Place of Birth

Special Interests

Grandfather's Full Name-6

Date of Birth   Place of Birth

Date of Marriage   Place of Marriage

Date of Death   Place of Burial

Occupation

Special Interests

Great Grandfather's Full Name-12

Date of Birth   Place of Birth

Occupation

Great Grandmother's Full Name-13

Date of Birth   Place of Birth

Special Interests

Grandmother's Full Name-7

Date of Birth   Place of Birth

Date of Marriage   Place of Marriage

Date of Death   Place of Burial

Occupation

Special Interests

Great Grandfather's Full Name-14

Date of Birth   Place of Birth

Occupation

Great Grandmother's Full Name-15

Date of Birth   Place of Birth

Special Interests

Anniversaries & Other Dates

Jan. | April
Name | Name
Occasion | Occasion

Feb. | May
Name | Name
Occasion | Occasion

March | June
Name | Name
Occasion | Occasion

Anniversaries & Other Dates

July

Name

Occasion

Oct.

Name

Occasion

Aug.

Name

Occasion

Nov.

Name

Occasion

Sept.

Name

Occasion

Dec.

Name

Occasion

Family Weddings

Date	Full Name	Married To

Date	Full Name	Married To

Date	Full Name	Married To

Date	Full Name	Married To

Date	Full Name	Married To

Date	Full Name	Married To

Divorces

Date	
	Full Name
	Divorced From
	Children
	Full Name
	Divorced From
	Children
	Full Name
	Divorced From
	Children
	Full Name
	Divorced From
	Children
	Full Name
	Divorced From
	Children
	Full Name
	Divorced From
	Children
	Full Name
	Divorced From
	Children
	Full Name
	Divorced From
	Children

Date	
	Full Name
	Remarried To
	Children
	Full Name
	Remarried To
	Children
	Full Name
	Remarried To
	Children
	Full Name
	Remarried To
	Children
	Full Name
	Remarried To
	Children
	Full Name
	Remarried To
	Children
	Full Name
	Remarried To
	Children
	Full Name
	Remarried To
	Children

Family Deaths

Date	Full Name	Relation	City	State

Family Deaths

Date	Full Name	Relation	City	State

Special Friends & Relatives

Name _____
Address _____
City _____ State _____ Zip _____
Telephone Area (   ) _____
Relation _____ Astrological Sign _____
Birth or Memorial Date _____

_____

Name _____
Address _____
City _____ State _____ Zip _____
Telephone Area (   ) _____
Relation _____ Astrological Sign _____
Birth or Memorial Date _____

_____

Name _____
Address _____
City _____ State _____ Zip _____
Telephone Area (   ) _____
Relation _____ Astrological Sign _____
Birth or Memorial Date _____

_____

Name _____
Address _____
City _____ State _____ Zip _____
Telephone Area (   ) _____
Relation _____ Astrological Sign _____
Birth or Memorial Date _____

_____

Name _____
Address _____
City _____ State _____ Zip _____
Telephone Area (   ) _____
Relation _____ Astrological Sign _____
Birth or Memorial Date _____

_____

Name _____
Address _____
City _____ State _____ Zip _____
Telephone Area (   ) _____
Relation _____ Astrological Sign _____
Birth or Memorial Date _____

_____

Name _____
Address _____
City _____ State _____ Zip _____
Telephone Area (   ) _____
Relation _____ Astrological Sign _____
Birth or Memorial Date _____

_____

Name _____
Address _____
City _____ State _____ Zip _____
Telephone Area (   ) _____
Relation _____ Astrological Sign _____
Birth or Memorial Date _____

_____

Special Friends & Relatives

Name_____
Address_____
City_____ State_____ Zip_____
Telephone Area (   )_____
Relation_____ Astrological Sign_____
Birth or Memorial Date _____
_____

Name_____
Address_____
City_____ State_____ Zip_____
Telephone Area (   )_____
Relation_____ Astrological Sign_____
Birth or Memorial Date _____
_____

Name_____
Address_____
City_____ State_____ Zip_____
Telephone Area (   )_____
Relation_____ Astrological Sign_____
Birth or Memorial Date _____
_____

Name_____
Address_____
City_____ State_____ Zip_____
Telephone Area (   )_____
Relation_____ Astrological Sign_____
Birth or Memorial Date _____
_____

Name_____
Address_____
City_____ State_____ Zip_____
Telephone Area (   )_____
Relation_____ Astrological Sign_____
Birth or Memorial Date _____
_____

Name_____
Address_____
City_____ State_____ Zip_____
Telephone Area (   )_____
Relation_____ Astrological Sign_____
Birth or Memorial Date _____
_____

Name_____
Address_____
City_____ State_____ Zip_____
Telephone Area (   )_____
Relation_____ Astrological Sign_____
Birth or Memorial Date _____
_____

Name_____
Address_____
City_____ State_____ Zip_____
Telephone Area (   )_____
Relation_____ Astrological Sign_____
Birth or Memorial Date _____
_____

Membership in Organizations

Professional · Fraternal · Clubs
Business · Religious · Community · Children's · Charities

Organization	Membership	
	From	To

Educational History

Grammar School

 School Name _____

 Address _____

 Dates Attended: From _____ To _____

_____

_____

_____

Junior High School

 School Name _____

 Address _____

 Dates Attended: From _____ To _____

_____

_____

_____

High School

 School Name _____

 Address _____

 Dates Attended: From _____ To _____

_____

_____

_____

College

 School Name _____

 Address _____

 Dates Attended: Major _____ Minor _____ Degree _____

 Achievements _____

_____

_____

_____

_____

_____

Military Service

Name_____ Branch of Service_____

Service Number_____ Rank_____

Time of Service: From_____ _____ _____   To _____ _____ _____
                              Month   Day   Year   Month   Day   Year

Specialty_____ Unit_____

Special Training: _____

_____

_____

Record of Service

Date	Rank	Place — Base, City, State, or Country

Awards and Commendations

Date	Place	Award or Commendation

Military Records Located At _____

_____

_____

_____

*T*he Veterans' Administration offers a wide range of benefits to those who have served their country in the Armed Forces and to their dependents. The following are only some of the highlights. Not all benefits are available if you enlisted the first time on or before September 8, 1980, and have not completed at least two years of active duty. Also, to qualify for benefits you must have been discharged under conditions other than dishonorable. For information, consult your telephone directory under United States Government, Veterans Administration. Toll-free telephone service is available in all 50 states.

Educational Assistance (GI Bill)—You may be eligible for educational benefits if you have at least 181 days of continuous active duty service which occured after January 31, 1955 and before January 1, 1977. Service personnel with 181 days or more of continuous active duty are also eligible. Eligibility generally ceases at the end of ten years from the date of your release or December 31, 1989, whichever is first.

Educational assistance covers counseling, change of program, farm cooperative training, and on-the-job training. The Veterans' Administration will not pay for educational assistance if the training costs are already being paid by the Federal Government.

Veterans have rights to their former jobs after completing active duty. If you enlisted, were drafted or recalled to active duty, you have a legal right to get your job back after discharge with seniority for the time spent in the service. You must apply within 90 days of your discharge.

Home Loan Benefits—Eligible veterans and service personnel may obtain a government guaranteed loan from private lenders for a home, lot, farm, and certain types of condominiums.

Veteran Administration Medical Care—The Veterans' Administration maintains hospitals throughout the United States as well as outpatient care when needed for all service-connected medical or compensated dental conditions.

Veteran Mortgage Life Insurance—You can buy life insurance at a special rate from the Veterans' Administration equal to your outstanding mortgage but not to exceed $40,000, whichever is less.

Reimbursement of Burial Expenses—The Veterans' Administration will pay $300 burial and funeral expenses plus a $150 plot or interment allowance.

Burial Flag—The Veterans' Administration will issue an American flag to drape the casket of an eligible veteran. Flags are issued by any VA office, VA national cemetery, and most local post offices.

Interment in National Cemeteries—The Veterans' Administration operates the National Cemetery System. Honorably discharged veterans and servicemen, a spouse, or minor children of an eligible veteran can be interred in a National Cemetery where space is available. There is no charge for a grave. A headstone or marker with inscription of each decedent is provided by the government.

For complete details and additional information, call your local Veterans' Administration Office.

Death

There is no such thing as death

In nature nothing dies

From each sad remnant of decay

Some forms of life arise.

Charles McKay

*M*edical genealogy is an invaluable record that could literally save a life. Most hereditary illnesses can be cured and controlled through early detection. An accurate family medical record can help your doctor detect early symptoms and prevent serious illness.

Illnesses are an unfortunate, yet unavoidable feature of life. It is important that you list all your serious illnesses on the following pages in chronological order. This documentation may be vital for future generations, especially to persons that may be at risk.

If you have had adverse reactions to certain medications, be sure to record this as a reminder to yourself and your doctor.

Because most of us tend to forget, it is important to record dates of immunizations. You should periodically reassess your immunization status and consult with your doctor about boosters and the development of influenza vaccines and other similar preventive measures.

Long life expectancy is a modern achievement. Preventive medicine is also helpful in reducing medical bills, as well as improving one's health.

Although medical care, disease control, and better nutrition have prolonged life expectancy, many doctors tell us that better health is based also on regular cardio-vascular exercise and recreation. They also believe there is a direct relationship between one's state of mind and physical health.

Those over forty years of age, in particular, nutritionists say, can not only assure themselves a longer life but a more enjoyable life, through such simple measures as a low-fat diet and regular exercise. Studies indicate that these two steps alone can in many instances slow, stop, or even reverse the aging process—or at least its physical aspects—including everything from

weight gain to bone decalcification.

Preventive care at any age, of course, is an important practice because it relies on one's knowledge of health maintenance through diet, exercise, annual checkups, consultation with a doctor and participation in community health screening for hypertension, glaucoma, diabetes, hearing and visual impairment, and heart disease.

Most people who feel well avoid checkups and consultations with their doctors, and therefore can be unaware of hypertension—which has no symptoms, but if left untreated can have serious consequences. Glaucoma is another condition which, if left untreated, can have very grave results but can easily be detected and treated by a doctor.

If you are facing surgery, consider getting a second opinion. This has become a standard, accepted medical practice. By law in most states, a patient is required to give his or her informed consent before any surgery is performed. In addition, a doctor must describe the alternatives available, their risks and benefits, and the length of incapacitation time for each alternative. Be sure to inquire about outpatient surgery. More and more these days it has become a viable alternative for less serious procedures—especially with its concomitant reduced cost and recuperation time.

The following pages provide an appropriate place to record your illnesses, operations and injuries, dates of immunizations and inoculations, reactions to various treatments and drugs. This information can be very helpful for your immediate family and very beneficial for future generations. Heredity plays an important part in the transference of susceptibility or resistance to certain diseases and malfunctions.

Medical History

Illnesses and medical problems believed to be genetically related:

- alcoholism
- allergies
- arthritis
- asthma
- atherosclerosis
- bacterial pneumonia
- birth defects
- cancers
- cysticfibrosis
- diabetes
- Down's syndrome
- dwarfism
- emphysema
- epilepsy
- hearing disorder
- heart attack
- hemophilia
- Huntington's disease
- high blood pressure
- liver diseases — like hepatitis
- systemic lupus erythematosos
- mental illness
- migraine headaches
- miscarriages
- multiple sclerosis
- muscular dystrophy
- myasthenia gravis
- obesity
- phenylketonuria
- RH disease
- sickle cell anemia
- skin disorders
- sudden infant death syndrome
- stroke
- suicide
- Tay-Sachs disease
- thyroid disorders
- tuberculosis
- visual disorders:
  cataracts, dyslexia, glaucoma,
  retinitis pigmentosis

SOURCE: MARCH OF DIMES

NAME _____

Date of Birth _____ Blood Type _____

Doctor _____

Visits _____

Date _____ Blood Pressure _____ Weight _____

_____

_____

_____

_____

_____

Date _____ Blood Test Results _____

_____

_____

_____

_____

_____

Date _____ Urine Test Results _____

_____

_____

_____

Doctor's Advice and Recommendations

_____

_____

_____

_____

_____

_____

_____

_____

Immunization and Dates Within Last Five Years

Date	Immunization	Booster Dates

Medical Prescriptions

Medication	From Date	To Date	Doctor	Telephone

Allergies _____

_____

Illnesses and Dates _____

_____

Reactions to Drugs

_____

Prescription Eyeglasses and Contact Lenses

Prescription	Date	Optometrist	Telephone

Medical History

Name _____ Date of Birth _____ Blood Type _____

Visits _____ Doctor _____

Date   Blood Pressure   Weight

_____

_____

_____

_____

_____

_____

Date   Blood Test Results   Doctor's Advice and Recommendations

_____

_____

_____

_____

_____

Date   Urine Test Results

_____

_____

_____

_____

_____

Allergies

_____

_____

Illnesses and Dates _____

_____

_____

_____

Immunization and Dates Within Last Five Years

Date   Immunization   Booster Dates

_____

_____

_____

_____

_____

_____

_____

Medical Prescriptions

Medication   From Date   To Date   Doctor   Telephone

_____

_____

_____

_____

_____

_____

_____

_____

Reactions to Drugs

_____

_____

_____

_____

_____

Prescription Eyeglasses and Contact Lenses

Prescription   Date   Optometrist   Telephone

_____

_____

_____

Medical History

Surgical Operations: _____ Doctor _____

Date _____ Hospital _____ City _____ State _____

X-rays Filed At _____

Test Results _____

Doctor's Advice and Instructions _____

_____

_____

_____

Comments _____

_____

_____

_____

_____

Surgical Operations: _____ Doctor _____

Date _____ Hospital _____ City _____ State _____

X-rays Filed At _____

Test Results _____

Doctor's Advice and Instructions _____

_____

_____

_____

Comments _____

_____

_____

_____

_____

*Visits*_____ *Doctor*_____

Date   *Blood Pressure*   *Weight*

_____

_____

_____

_____

_____

_____

Date   *Blood Test Results*   *Doctor's Advice and Recommendations*

_____

_____

_____

_____

_____

Date   *Urine Test Results*

_____

_____

_____

_____

_____

Allergies

_____

_____

*Illnesses and Dates*_____

_____

_____

_____

Vital Papers

*T*he word vital means "relating to life." Vital papers, therefore, document key moments in our life histories: our birth certificates, confirmation or baptismal certificates, and marriage certificates. In addition, there are innumerable papers that record other significant events. A diploma, an armed services discharge, naturalization papers, real estate deeds—every step we take is registered by some branch of government on a piece of paper. By the time you take up this book you will probably have accumulated more documents than you realize.

These documents are often lost or misplaced. Gathering them together, keeping them together, keeping them in order and in a safe place, is one of the most important things you can do for yourself and for your family. This kind of record-keeping will help you analyze your assets and rights. And when you are no longer here, your vital papers must speak for you. In the future, your family may have to produce these papers quickly in order to settle your estate efficiently, to properly document business and insurance claims, or Social Security and Veteran's benefits.

Once you have brought the papers together, find a secure place for them. A bank safe-deposit box is the best protection against damage or theft. (If you decide to keep your papers at home, use a locked, fireproof metal box.) Indicate the location of the deposit box and the key. If your family doesn't know where your papers are kept and lengthly search has to be made, precious time will be lost. Consider giving another family member title to the safe-deposit box so that it can be opened without a court order.

You may not always need to have your vital papers actually in hand. Occasions will arise when you simply require some information from them—a registration or policy number, for example, or a specific date and place, or the name and address of an agent or company. Record such facts here to have convenient access to them, without making a trip to the bank or working through a pile of documents. And your family will be able to see at a glance what papers are available and what information they contain.

Nothing is more vital to the welfare of your family than a properly prepared will. Without a will, the court determines the disposition of your assets according to law. It will appoint an executor to oversee your estate. This person may not make the same decisions you would. Moreover, the law acts impersonally. No allowance is made for indivdual circumstances: in distributing your assets, the law does not consider that one of your heirs may be needier than another, or may have a special claim to part of your property. Only by making a will can you control these matters and be assured that your wishes are carried out. If you do not yet have a will, the time to make one is now. A delay may cause your loved ones unnecessary problems. Perhaps you've put it off because the facts and figures needed seem difficult to assemble. This book not only provides guidelines for preparing a will, but it will help you organize your records and itemize your property. In this way, you can form a detailed picture of your estate. If you already have a will, look it over and make sure that all your assets and heirs are specified and that it follows the directions set forth in the guidelines. Review the will periodically to see if it still accords with your wishes.

The Importance of a Will

A properly prepared will is one of the most important gifts you can provide for your family. It is the single most important legal document affecting a family's future. It instructs others about the disposition of your property and assets after your death. If you die without a will, or if your will does not conform with existing state laws, all your property and assets will be distributed by the court according to the laws of the state in which you live, with no regard whatsoever for the needs of your heirs.

Many young couples—and some older ones—make the mistake of thinking that because they have a modest estate they do not need a will. But let's say a couple is renting an apartment, and has few assets except for their household effects, their clothes, and their car. If both die in the same accident and it is established that a third party caused their deaths, the resulting lawsuit could net their heirs considerable money—but only if a valid will indicated that their modest estate be left to these heirs.

A will should be drawn up with a thorough, up-to-date knowledge of existing state laws, as well as of federal inheritance and gift taxes. Your permanent residence determines which state laws apply. Should you own property or have a bank account in another state, or if your will does not conform with the state's laws, your property and assets will be distributed as if there were no will.

There are a variety of ways in which an estate can be dispersed. A member of your family may have specific needs. Perhaps you wish to disinherit a member of your family; or you may want to assure that a potential heir not get more than his or her share.

Appoint as executor of your estate a person whom you trust and who is capable of handling the responsibility of managing your estate after your death. It can be your spouse, adult child, or a friend. You should appoint an alternate executor in the event of the death or incapacitation of the individual who is your first choice. Your executor should be available over an extended period of time.

Among an executor's wide-ranging catalog of duties are: 1) setting up a checking account; 2) taking inventory of all safe-deposit box contents; 3) publishing a notice of his appointment as executor in local newspapers; 4) obtaining appraisals of all real estate and valuable personal property items, and insuring the latter; 5) processing all insurance claims, and applying for all applicable benefits; 6) paying all estate bills, taxes, and claims; 7) accounting to the probate court for all transactions handled on behalf of the estate; 8) distributing all property to heirs as designated, and obtaining receipts for verification.

It is important to have an itemized account of all your obvious assets, such as bank accounts, insurance policies, jewelry, real estate, family heirlooms, stocks and bonds, paintings, valuable collections, family documents, and items of sentimental value. This book, when completed, will contain all the necessary information about the contents of your estate in one convenient place.

Be sure to list all your beneficiaries' names and addresses, whether individuals or organizations, so that they can be located and properly identified. Include any additional information that might be needed in the case of distant relatives or friends.

When considering the distribution of your stocks and bonds, keep in mind that their value may fluctuate. Perhaps unforeseen financial reverses may cause problems after a will is written. To avoid the effects of unexpected net worth changes, allocate percentages rather than specific dollar amounts.

How to Write Your Own Will

*U*ntil just a few years ago, the preparation of one's will without legal assistance was strongly discouraged—particularly (and understandably) by the legal community itself. Now, however, self-help kits enabling individuals to write their own wills are available nationwide, and are perfectly legal—provided both federal and state laws are followed.

This is a particularly critical proviso, however, because if such laws are deviated from even in the slightest, or if you are not precise enough in the language you use to fill in the blanks, a will you wrote could be declared invalid after your death, and your property would be divided according to state law rather than reflect your wishes. And because it is impossible for a lay person to remain up to date on all state legislation that may affect the preparation of a will and the distribution of an estate, it may be a good idea to ask a lawyer to review any will you write to insure that all recent legislation has been taken into consideration.

Most couples write separate rather than joint wills. One reason is that in the 1990s nearly as many couples are experiencing their second or third marriages as those who have married only once. Both husband and wife are likely to have children from earlier marriages, in addition, perhaps, one or more children together. For this reason—as well as the fact that each party probably brought some of his or her own property into the relationship—writing a will today can be more complex than it was a generation ago. Joint wills in most instances need to allow for too many contingencies to be useful. It is usually simpler and just as economical to prepare separate wills.

First step is to query various members of your family to determine specific needs they have that you may not have been aware of, or to find out what family and individual situations may have changed without your knowledge—to the extent that you are able to alter or improve any given situation. Through this simple method you also can learn what heirlooms, artifacts, or other items of value not previously accounted for are of interest to whom, so that they can be allocated equitably with minimum recrimination.

Next, contact your local congressional representative, and ask for copies of all recent state legislation related to wills and estate planning. This way you can keep up with change made in relevant law that may affect the way you write your will.

Among other points to consider when drawing up your will are these:

- Is it likely that you will have or adopt additional children, and if so, how will they be provided for?
- If you have young children, who will be appointed as their guardians?
- Do you want any stepchildren to share in your estate?
- Will your spouse have complete freedom to dispose of your property if he or she remarries?
- If assets must be sold to pay your debts, do you want to designate the sequence in which each is to be paid?
- Who is to receive the remainder of your estate after all specific bequests have been made?
- Do you want to cancel debts owed you by your heirs, or should they be deducted from their inheritances?

When signing your will it is very important that your signature is witnessed by three adults. Your witnesses can not be beneficiaries named in your will. All three witnesses must also sign your will in your presence as well as in the presence of each other. Each witness must state their full name and address. It is not necessary for anyone to read the contents of your will. All previous wills should be destroyed.

Last Will and Testament

I, _____ *(Your full name)* _____ residing at _____ *(Street Address)* _____

City of _____ , State of _____

being of sound mind, I do hereby declare this instrument to be my last Will and Testament and do hereby revoke any and all other Wills and Codicils made by me.

I. I order and direct my Executor to pay my just debts, obligations and funeral expenses and to carry out all provisions of this Will, as soon after my death as may be practical.

II. I am a _____ *(single or married)* _____ person. My spouse is _____ *(If single N/A)* _____ and

_____ *(Names of children)* _____ ,

are all my children either natural or adopted.

III. I nominate my spouse as Guardian of my minor children. In the event that my spouse shall predecease me or fails to serve as such Guardian, I then appoint

_____ *(Name of guardian)* _____ Guardian of the person and property of my minor children. I further direct that no bond shall be required for the performance of his/her duties.

IV. I hereby make the following specific bequests:

(use as much space as necessary to list all your bequests)

V. I hereby bequeath all remainder of my estate to dispose to _____ *(Name)* _____

VI. I have appointed _____ *(Name of executor)* _____ as Executor of this Will. In the event that the Executor named above shall predecease me or

fails to serve as such Executor of this Will, I appoint _____ *(Alternate Executor)* as Executor I further direct that no appointee shall be required to post surety bond for the performance of their duties.

continued

Last Will and Testament

IIV. I hereby authorize my Executor to exercise all power, rights, discretion and duties deemed necessary for the proper administration and disposition of my estate that is permitted by law.

I subscribe my name to this Will this _____ *Day of* _____*(month)*_____ *, 19*_____ *at*

_____ , _____

City   State

_____*(Your signature)*_____

Signature

On the day written below, _____*(Your full name)*_____

*declared to us, the undersigned that this instrument, consisting of #*_____ *pages, was*

__*(His/Her)*__ *Will and* __*(He/She)*__ *requested us to act as witness to it.* __*(He/She)*__ *thereupon signed this Will in our presence, all of us being present at the same time. We now in* __*(His or Her)*__ *presence and in the presence of each other subscribe our names as witnesses.*

It is our belief that _____*(Your full name)*_____ *is of sound mind and under no constraint or undue influence whatsoever.*

We declare under penalty of perjury that the foregoing is true and correct and that

this declaration was executed on _____ *, 19* _____ *,*

at _____*(City)*_____ _____*(State)*_____

_____ _____

Witness   Address

_____ _____

Witness   Address

_____ _____

Witness   Address

As a final step you may wish to have your Will notarized by a Notary Public.

Will

What The Family Should Know

Date _____   Date _____

Name _____   Name _____

Location of Will _____   Location of Will _____

Name of Attorney _____   Name of Attorney _____

Address _____   Address _____

City _____ State _____   City _____ State _____

          Zip _____   Zip _____

Telephone _____   Telephone _____

Name of Witnesses   Telephone   Name of Witnesses   Telephone

_____   _____

_____   _____

_____   _____

Name of Executor _____   Name of Executor _____

Address _____   Address _____

City _____ State _____   City _____ State _____

          Zip _____   Zip _____

Telephone _____   Telephone _____

Alternate Executor _____   Alternate Executor _____

Name _____   Name _____

Address _____   Address _____

City _____ State _____   City _____ State _____

          Zip _____   Zip _____

Telephone _____   Telephone _____

Date _____   Date _____

Are there amendments to the above will: ____   Are there amendments to the above will: ____

_____   _____

Signature _____   Signature _____

The Living Will and How to Write One

A "Living Will" is a voluntary document drawn up in advance by an individual declaring that he or she does not want life artificially prolonged after the doctor says there is no hope for recovery. It gives an individual the right to die with dignity—a "natural" death. A Living Will instructs doctors to withhold or withdraw life-support equipment (mechanical respiration and intravenous feeding, for example) when an individual is too ill to communicate these thoughts, and relieves relatives of the responsibility of making this decision themselves.

Forty one states and the District of Columbia have passed legislation that recognizes the legitimacy of the Living Will, and indicates under what circumstances this document is valid and the extent to which it can be implemented. Most states specify that to prepare a valid Living Will one must be at least 18 years of age. In some states restrictions are made precluding relatives, or beneficiaries to a person's estate, to act as witnesses. The way these laws have been written varies in other ways as well from state to state, so it is wise to find out exactly what limitations and exigencies exist where you live.

Even in states where there are no Living Will laws, it may be wise to prepare one. For one thing, such a law ultimately may be passed. For another, at least your wishes are expressed on paper in the event that a situation arises that would cause your spouse or another relative to act on them.

After you write your Living Will, give copies to everyone in your family, as well as your doctor and attorney. Be sure they understand your intent, and agree to abide by it. Those who don't, you'll know to replace accordingly. A national repository for information on Living Wills is the Society For The Right To Die 250 W. 57th Street, Suite 323, New York,

NY 10107, (212) 246-6973. This is a national nonprofit organization that provides, in addition to Living Will forms and instructions compatible in all 50 states, legal and medical counseling, an attorney and doctor referral service, and an educational publications division including handbooks, pamphlets, a newsletter published three times a year, and a legal subscription service consisting of fact sheets on all major right-to-die cases in states where they have occurred.

Keep in mind that if you move to another state after completing a Living Will, you may have to write another one. As of our press date only Maine, Maryland, and Montana honored Living Wills prepared outside their states.

Your signature on your Living Will must be witnessed by three adults. Your witnesses can not be beneficiaries. All three witnesses must also sign your Living Will in your presence as well as in the presence of each other. Each witness must state their full name and address.

HEALTH CARE POWERS of ATTORNEY

In addition to your Living Will it is also recommended that you have a Health Care Powers of Attorney document. It's a legal form authorizing a person you designate to act in your behalf in the event you become temporarily or permanently disabled, incompetent and unable to speak for yourself. This document can contain instructions in regard to your wishes and preferences regarding specific medical decisions. Without this document the health care provider or institution will make critical decisions for you which may be contrary to what you want.

Please remember that every person's situation is different, and laws vary from state to state. For Up-to-date information on Health Care Powers of Attorney and Living Will forms for your state can be obtained from Society For The Right To Die at the above address.

Living Will Declaration

To My Family, Doctors, and All Those Concerned with My Care.

I, _____ , being of sound mind, make this statement as a directive to be followed if I become unable to participate in decisions regarding my medical care.

If I should be in an incurable or irreversible mental or physical condition with no reasonable expectation of recovery, I direct my attending physician to withhold or withdraw treatment that merely prolongs my dying. I further direct that treatment be limited to measures to keep me comfortable and to relieve pain.

These directions express my legal right to refuse treatment. Therefore I expect my family, doctors, and everyone concerned with my care to regard themselves as legally and morally bound to act in accord with my wishes, and in so doing to be free of any legal liability for having followed my directions.

I especially do not want: _____

_____

Note: You may list specific treatment you do not want. For example: cardiac resuscitation, mechanical respiration, artificial feeding/fluids by tube.

Other instructions/comments: _____

_____

Note: You may want to add instructions for care you do want—for example, pain medication, or that you prefer to die at home if possible.

Proxy Designation Clause: Should I become unable to communicate my instructions as stated above, I designate the following person to act in my behalf:

Name _____

Address _____

If the person I have named above is unable to act on my behalf, I authorize the following person to do so:

Name _____

Address _____

Signed: _____ Date: _____

Witness: _____ Address: _____

Witness: _____ Address: _____

Keep the signed original with your personal papers at home. Give signed copies to doctors, family, and proxy. Review your Declaration from time to time; initial and date it to show it still expresses your intent.

Power of Attorney for Health Care

(NOTICE: THE PURPOSE OF THIS POWER OF ATTORNEY IS TO GIVE THE PERSON YOU DESIGNATE (YOUR "AGENT") BROAD POWERS TO MAKE HEALTH CARE DECISIONS FOR YOU, INCLUDING POWER TO REQUIRE, CONSENT TO OR WITHDRAW ANY TYPE OF PERSONAL CARE OR MEDICAL TREATMENT FOR ANY PHYSICAL OR MENTAL CONDITION AND TO ADMIT YOU TO OR DISCHARGE YOU FROM ANY HOSPITAL, HOME OR OTHER INSTITUTION. THIS FORM DOES NOT IMPOSE A DUTY ON YOUR AGENT TO EXERCISE GRANTED POWERS: BUT WHEN A POWER IS EXERCISED, YOUR AGENT WILL HAVE TO USE DUE CARE TO ACT FOR YOUR BENEFIT AND IN ACCORDANCE WITH THIS FORM. A COURT CAN TAKE AWAY THE POWERS OF YOUR AGENT IF IT FINDS THE AGENT IS NOT ACTING PROPERLY. YOU MAY NAME SUCCESSOR AGENTS UNDER THIS FORM BUT NOT CO-AGENTS, AND NO HEALTH CARE PROVIDER MAY BE NAMED. UNLESS YOU EXPRESSLY LIMIT THE DURATION OF THIS POWER IN THE MANNER PROVIDED BELOW, UNTIL YOU REVOKE THIS POWER OR A COURT ACTING ON YOUR BEHALF TERMINATES IT, YOUR AGENT MAY EXERCISE THE POWERS GIVEN HERE THROUGHOUT YOUR LIFETIME, EVEN AFTER YOU BECOME DISABLED. THE POWERS YOU GIVE YOUR AGENT, YOUR RIGHT TO REVOKE THOSE POWERS AND THE PENALTIES FOR VIOLATING THE LAW ARE EXPLAINED MORE FULLY IN "POWERS OF ATTORNEY FOR HEALTH CARE LAW". THAT LAW EXPRESSLY PERMITS THE USE OF ANY DIFFERENT FORM OF POWER OF ATTORNEY YOU MAY DESIRE. IF THERE IS ANYTHING THAT YOU DO NOT UNDERSTAND, YOU SHOULD ASK A LAWYER TO EXPLAIN IT TO YOU.)

POWER OF ATTORNEY made this _____ day _____
                                             (month)   (year)

1. I, _____,
                       (insert name and address of principal)

hereby appoint:

_____
                       (insert name and address of agent)

as my attorney-in-fact (my "agent") to act for me and in my name (in any way I could act in person) to make any and all decisions for me concerning my personal care, medical treatment, hospitalization and health care and to require, withold or withdraw any type of medical treatment or procedure, even though my death may ensue. My agent shall have the same access to my medical records that I have, including the right to disclose the contents to others. My agent shall also have full power to make a disposition of any part or all of my body for medical purposes, authorize an autopsy and direct the disposition of my remains.

(THE ABOVE GRANT OF POWER IS INTENDED TO BE AS BROAD AS POSSIBLE SO THAT YOUR AGENT WILL HAVE AUTHORITY TO MAKE ANY DECISION YOU COULD MAKE TO OBTAIN OR TERMINATE ANY TYPE OF HEALTH CARE, INCLUDING WITHDRAWAL OF FOOD AND WATER AND OTHER LIFE-SUSTAINING MEASURES, IF YOUR AGENT BELIEVES SUCH ACTION WOULD BE CONSISTENT WITH YOUR INTENT AND DESIRES. IF YOU WISH TO LIMIT THE SCOPE OF YOUR AGENT'S POWERS OR PRESCRIBE SPECIAL RULES OR LIMIT THE POWER TO MAKE AN ANATOMICAL GIFT, AUTHORIZE AUTOPSY OR DISPOSE OF REMAINS, YOU MAY DO SO IN THE FOLLOWING PARAGRAPHS.)

2. The powers granted above shall not include the following powers or shall be subject to the following rules or limitations (here you may include any specific limitations you deem appropriate, such as: your own definition of when life-sustaining measures should be withheld; a direction to continue food and fluids or life-sustaining treatment in all events; or instructions to refuse any specific types of treatment that are inconsistent with your religious beliefs or unacceptable to you for any other reason, such as blood transfusion, electro-convulsive therapy, amputation, psychosurgery, voluntary admission to a mental institution, etc.):

_____

_____

_____

_____

Power of Attorney for Health Care

(THE SUBJECT OF LIFE-SUSTAINING TREATMENT IS OF PARTICULAR IMPORTANCE. FOR YOUR CONVENIENCE IN DEALING WITH THAT SUBJECT, SOME GENERAL STATEMENTS CONCERNING THE WITHHOLDING OR REMOVAL OF LIFE-SUSTAINING TREATMENT ARE SET FORTH BELOW. IF YOU AGREE WITH ONE OF THESE STATEMENTS, YOU MAY INITIAL THAT STATEMENT; BUT DO NOT INITIAL MORE THAN ONE):

I do not want my life to be prolonged nor do I want life-sustaining treatment to be provided or continued if my agent believes the burdens of the treatment outweigh the expected benefits. I want my agent to consider the relief of suffering, the expense involved and the quality as well as the possible extension of my life in making decisions concerning life-sustaining treatment.

Inital _____

I want my life to be prolonged and I want life-sustaining treatment to be provided or continued unless I am in a coma which my attending physician believes to be irreversible, in accordance with reasonable medical standards at the time of reference. If and when I have suffered irreversible coma, I want life-sustaining treatment to be withheld or discontinued.

Initial _____

I want my life to be prolonged to the greatest extent possible without regard to my condition, the chances I have for recovery or the cost of the procedures.

Initial _____

(THIS POWER OF ATTORNEY MAY BE AMENDED OR REVOKED BY YOU AT ANY TIME AND IN ANY MANNER WHILE YOU HAVE THE CAPACITY TO DO SO. ABSENT AMENDMENT OR REVOCATION, THE AUTHORITY GRANTED IN THIS POWER OF ATTORNEY WILL BECOME EFFECTIVE AT THE TIME THIS POWER IS SIGNED AND WILL CONTINUE UNTIL YOUR DEATH, AND BEYOND IF ANATOMICAL GIFT, AUTOPSY OR DISPOSITION OF REMAINS IS AUTHORIZED, UNLESS A LIMITATION ON THE BEGINNING DATE OR DURATION IS MADE BY INITIALING AND COMPLETING EITHER OR BOTH OF THE FOLLOWING:)

3. (   ) This power of attorney shall become effective on _____

_____

(insert a future date or event during your lifetime, such as court determination of your disability, when you want this power to first take effect)

4. (   ) This power of attorney shall terminate on

_____

(insert a future date or event, such as court determination of your disability, when you want this power to terminated prior to your death)

(IF YOU WISH TO NAME SUCCESSOR AGENTS, INSERT THE NAMES AND ADDRESSES OF SUCH SUCCESSORS IN THE FOLLOWING PARAGRAPH.)

5. If any agent named by me shall die, become legally disabled, resign, refuse to act or be unavailable, I name the following (each to act alone and successively, in the order named) as successors to such agent:

_____

_____

(IF YOU WISH TO NAME A GUARDIAN OF YOUR PERSON IN THE EVENT A COURT DECIDES THAT ONE SHOULD BE APPOINTED, YOU MAY, BUT ARE NOT REQUIRED TO, DO SO BY INSERTING THE NAME OF SUCH GUARDIAN IN THE FOLLOWING PARAGRAPH. THE COURT WILL APPOINT THE PERSON NOMINATED BY YOU IF THE COURT FINDS THAT SUCH APPOINTMENT WILL SERVE YOUR BEST INTERESTS AND WELFARE. YOU MAY, BUT ARE NOT REQUIRED TO, NOMINATE AS YOUR GUARDIAN THE SAME PERSON NAMED IN THIS FORM AS YOUR AGENT.)

continued

6. If a guardian of my person is to be appointed, I nominate the following to serve as such guardian:

_____

_____

(insert name and address of nominated guardian of the person)

7. I am fully informed as to all the contents of this form and understand in full the importance of this grant of powers to my agent.

Signed _____

(principal)

The principal has had an opportunity to read the above form and has signed the form or acknowledged his or her signature or mark on the form in my presence.

_____ Residing at _____
(witness)

_____

(YOU MAY, BUT ARE NOT REQUIRED TO, REQUEST YOUR AGENT AND SUCCESSOR AGENTS TO PROVIDE SPECIMEN SIGNATURES BELOW. IF YOU INCLUDE SPECIMEN SIGNATURES IN THIS POWER OF ATTORNEY, YOU MUST COMPLETE THE CERTIFICATION OPPOSITE THE SIGNATURE OF THE AGENTS.)

Specimen signatures of agent (and successors).

I certify that signatures of my agent (and successors) are correct.

_____   _____
(agent)   (principal)

_____   _____
(agent)   (principal)

_____   _____
(agent)   (principal)

CAUTIONS

Laws and regulations vary from state to state and are subject to different interpretations. Some state laws specify witness requirements and restrictions as to whom you can and can't appoint as your agent. Some states that have such rules are; Alaska, California, the District of Columbia, Idaho, Kansas, Illinois, Nevada, Oregon, Rhode Island, Texas, Utah and Vermont.

Even where witnesses are not required or where a legal status is uncertain, it is still important to have something in writing because it carries a "moral weight." Your personal written directives cannot be easily ignored by your family or courts should they become involved in a dispute over preferences that you have expressed in writing; especially if your directive is signed by witnesses and your signature is notarized.

Please note; legal forms may not meet all of your individual needs. Take time to consider all possibilities and find competent advise, so that the document you develop meets all your special needs.

You can terminate, change your mind, revise and update any document, at anytime, that you develop. Remember to destroy all old documents that have been terminated or revised.

Passports

My Passport No. _____ Issue Date _____ Expiration Date _____

Place of Issue _____ City _____ State _____

Location of Passport _____

_____

Immunizations Received:

Date	Description	Administered By

Dates and Countries Traveled To: _____

_____

_____

_____

_____

_____

_____

_____

_____

_____

_____

_____

_____

_____

_____

_____

_____

_____

Other Vital Documents

Date	Summary of Document	Location
	Your Birth Certificate	
	Your Wife's Birth Certificate	
	Children's Birth Certificates	
	Adoption Records	
	Citizenship	
	Marriage Certificates	
	Pre-nuptial Agreement	
	Social Security Card	
	Your Wife's Social Security Card #	
	Separation Papers	
	Divorce Records	
	Military Discharge Papers	
	Other	

Wallet Contents

Driver's License No. _____ Expiration Date _____

Credit Cards _____

_____

Checks _____

_____

Cash _____

_____

Personal I.D. _____

_____

_____

Credit Card Data

Name of Charge Card	Account Number	Annual Fee	Credit Line	Expiration Date	Telephone No.

Insurance Policies

Almost everyone is covered by some form of insurance. Indeed, most of us have policies that protect our property and our lives from cradle to grave—accident, illness, old age and, of course, "life" insurance. However, it is often hard to keep track of who is covering you and exactly what kind of coverage it is. You may have taken out policies as an individual, or joined up with a plan through an organization or your place of business. Some forms of insurance are automatically provided by an employer or—as with the armed forces—by the government. Many people don't know that they have such policies and therefore never claim benefits to which they or their families are entitled. And don't forget that salary deductions are a kind of insurance premium too, for it is out of these taxes that the government distributes workmen's compensation, disability, unemployment and Social Security benefits.

You and your family should keep a careful account of all insurance coverage, what the benefits are, to whom they can be paid, and under what circumstances. Such information is essential if premium payments are to be kept up-to-date and if your heirs are to make the proper claims. And in order to estimate the value of your estate, you should know which policies pay benefits at your death and which ones will be canceled. Your family must also be told about those policies, such as property insurance, which they will have to continue.

Begin by taking a survey of all your coverage, using the categories outlined in this section. The picture may vary according to your interests, assets, and employment situation. When you have brought the policies together, read through them to check whether they are still current and what benefits they pay. An insurance agent may provide valuable assistance here. In the pages that follow, explanations of different kinds of insurance are given. You may want to consider taking out more insurance where you find your coverage too limited.

An insurance policy is a troublesome and sometimes costly piece of paper to replace. All such documents should be kept in a safe-deposit box with the rest of your vital papers. You do not need the policy itself in order to file a claim or check the extent of your coverage. Use this section to enter the pertinent information about each policy—description of coverage, name and address of the insurance company or agent, policy number, beneficiaries, special terms, and so forth. The result will be a convenient reference book for you and an essential record for your heirs. They will know which agent to contact for each policy and what the policy covers. If your heirs have to sort through unfamiliar papers to determine what benefits they are owed, they may inadvertently pass over an important clause and neglect to file a claim. Protect their rights.

It is a little known fact that a lost or misplaced life insurance policy can be tracked down by writing to:

Policy Search Department of the American Council of Life Insurance
1850 K Street, N.W., Washington, DC 20006

You should include as many details as possible, Social Security number, full name (maiden name where applicable), birth date, current and past addresses. This information is sent to over 150 insurance companies throughout the United States to check on whether or not a life insurance policy was issued.

Oftentimes a life insurance policy is paid in full and then misplaced. After the insured dies, family members often recall discussions of life insurance, but are unable to locate the policy or any record of it. You can perhaps solve the mystery by writing to the Council. It is a free service.

*I*nsurance is a form of security against uncertainties in life.

Following are basic types and forms of insurance by which most of us are covered:

Business Insurance—A few examples of the many types are Business Interruption Insurance, Credit Insurance, Insurance on Goods in Transit and in Storage, Key Executive Insurance on the Lives of Partners, Marine Insurance, Product Liability Floaters, Sprinkler Leakage, Water Damage, Malpractice, etc.

Comprehensive Home Insurance Policy—This is a package type of policy that provides a range of protection in one single policy which is less expensive than buying individual policies.

Credit Life Insurance—Covers all personal debts in the event you die before completing your payments.

Decreasing Term Insurance—This type of policy provides larger benefits in the beginning which gradually decrease to zero. Premiums remain the same throughout. Term insurance has the lowest premiums because it has no cash surrender value and the insured cannot borrow against the policy.

Endowment Policy—Is life insurance that can be collected personally while the insured is still alive. Should you die before the policy matures, the proceeds are paid to your beneficiary. The endowment policy is like the limited payment life insurance whereby premiums are paid within a specific time period or up to a specific age.

Group Health Insurance—This form of insurance is made available to employees by employers, labor unions and professional organizations. The insurance is terminated when you leave the company; however, in most situations the group insurance policy can be converted to an individual policy.

Group Life Insurance—This form of insurance is offered by most companies to their employees as well as by trade unions to their members. Generally, the face amount of insurance equals the employee's annual earnings and the employer picks up the entire cost.

Homeowners Policy—Covers your home and contents and all structures on your property. This policy also provides coverage for personal liability against lawsuits or a claim.

Hospitalization Insurance—Blue Cross is perhaps the most familiar example. This insurance provides payment for room and board, general nursing care in a semi-private rooms for a specific number of days.

Life Insurance Trust—This is an arrangement with a bank or a trust company whereby your life insurance assets are entrusted to be professionally managed for the beneficiary. The trustee 'invests the funds and pays them out in installments to the beneficiary. This method provides security to your heirs for a long period of time.

Limited Payment Life Insurance—Has all the benefits of a whole life policy. The difference is that you pay premiums for a specific number of years. The advantage is that you accumulate a larger cash value at an earlier age and you remain insured for the rest of your life.

Major Medical Insurance—This insurance provides you with continued protection where Blue Cross and Blue Shield stop once maximum coverage is reached. This is an important policy in the event of prolonged or chronic illness.

Medicare—Is administered by the Federal Government. It is a part of the social security program. Medicare covers hospitalization and medical benefits for most people sixty-five and older.

Mortgage Insurance—This policy insures payments on the mortgage on your house should you die. The policy runs the term of your mort-

Insurance Policies

gage. At death proceeds can be paid in one lump sum to the beneficiary or in monthly installments equal to monthly mortgage payments until the entire mortgage is paid in full.

***Federal Deposit Insurance**—The depositor is insured up to a specified amount in the event the bank should fail.*

***Floater**—Is a policy that protects your property wherever you take it or send it. Articles of particular value such as antiques, furs, jewelry, paintings, collections as well as securities should be listed separately from your homeowners policy because each should be insured for its actual value. A homeowners policy provides only very limited coverage on items of particular value. Personal effects that you carry when you travel can also be insured by a floater policy.*

***Fraternal Insurance Contracts**—Many fraternities form their own insurance companies for the benefit of their members. Their policies are similar to the private and commercial companies. The only difference is that the fraternal insurance is part of the fraternal charter and its constitution.*

***General Liability Insurance**—If you are operating a business, this type of policy will protect you against physical injury that may occur to others as well as damage to their property. This policy provides a legal defense plus payment in damages to the extent covered by the policy. If you are a landlord and/or own business property or an apartment, you should cover yourself against claims from tenants as well as visitors who enter your property.*

***GI and Veteran Life Insurance**—Whoever served in the United States Armed Forces during World War I, World War II and the Korean War was offered government-sponsored life insurance at very low cost. Armed services still have government-sponsored insurance. Contact your Veterans Administration for details.*

***Personal Liability Insurance**—This type policy provides you with protection in the event either you or a member of your family is responsible for property damage, accident or bodily injury to someone else. The policy covers fees for legal defense and damages up to the value of the policy in any act of negligence that may occur on your property. This coverage is normally bought with your homeowners policy.*

***Renewable Term Insurance**—You can renew this policy when it expires without retaking a medical exam. Premiums will be higher because of age.*

***Retirement Insurance**—This may be a combination of the following: Social Security, company pension plan, tax sheltered retirement plans such as Keogh for self-employed persons or IRA (Individual Retirement Account), an annuity or a retirement endowment policy.*

***Split-Dollar Insurance**—This type policy is often set up to enable an employee to share his cost of insurance with his employer when the employee elects to take out a larger policy. Generally the employer pays only part of the premium proportionate to the increased value of the policy. If the employee dies, the employer gets back the amount that he paid in.*

***Term Life Insurance**—This policy provides protection for a specific time period. When the policy expires it has no cash value as does whole life insurance.*

Individual Life

Name of Insured _____

Name of Insurance Company _____

Agent's Name _____ Phone No. _____

Address _____ City _____ State _____

Type of Insurance _____ Policy No. _____

Issue Date _____ Expiration Date _____

Total Death Benefits _____ Cash Value _____

Beneficiary _____ Policy Owner _____

Premiums Paid Annually _____ Monthly _____

Office to Which Premiums Are Paid _____

Location of Policy _____

Name of Insured _____

Name of Insurance Company _____

Agent's Name _____ Phone No. _____

Address _____ City _____ State _____

Type of Insurance _____ Policy No. _____

Issue Date _____ Expiration Date _____

Total Death Benefits _____ Cash Value _____

Beneficiary _____ Policy Owner _____

Premiums Paid Annually _____ Monthly _____

Office to Which Premiums Are Paid _____

Location of Policy _____

Comments: _____

_____

_____

_____

_____

_____

_____

_____

Individual Life

Name of Insured _____

Name of Insurance Company _____

Agent's Name _____   Phone No. _____

Address _____   City _____ State _____

Type of Insurance _____   Policy No. _____

Issue Date _____   Expiration Date _____

Total Death Benefits _____   Cash Value _____

Beneficiary _____   Policy Owner _____

Premiums Paid Annually _____   Monthly _____

Office to Which Premiums Are Paid _____

Location of Policy _____

Name of Insured _____

Name of Insurance Company _____

Agent's Name _____   Phone No. _____

Address _____   City _____ State _____

Type of Insurance _____   Policy No. _____

Issue Date _____   Expiration Date _____

Total Death Benefits _____   Cash Value _____

Beneficiary _____   Policy Owner _____

Premiums Paid Annually _____   Monthly _____

Office to Which Premiums Are Paid _____

Location of Policy _____

Comments: _____

_____

_____

_____

_____

_____

_____

_____

Name of Insured _____

Name of Insurance Company _____

Agent's Name _____ Phone No. _____

Address _____ City _____ State _____

Type of Insurance _____ Policy No. _____

Issue Date _____ Expiration Date _____

Total Death Benefits _____ Cash Value _____

Beneficiary _____ Policy Owner _____

Premiums Paid Annually _____ Monthly _____

Office to Which Premiums Are Paid _____

Location of Policy _____

Name of Insured _____

Name of Insurance Company _____

Agent's Name _____ Phone No. _____

Address _____ City _____ State _____

Type of Insurance _____ Policy No. _____

Issue Date _____ Expiration Date _____

Total Death Benefits _____ Cash Value _____

Beneficiary _____ Policy Owner _____

Premiums Paid Annually _____ Monthly _____

Office to Which Premiums Are Paid _____

Location of Policy _____

Comments: _____

_____

_____

_____

_____

_____

_____

Accident & Health

Type of Policy _____

Name of Insurance Company _____ Policy No. _____

Agent's Name _____ Phone No. _____

Address _____

City _____ State _____ Zip _____

Issue Date _____ Expiration Date _____

Premiums Paid Annually _____ Monthly _____

Office to Which Premiums Are Paid _____

Benefits Provided _____ Policy Owner _____

Location of Policy _____

Persons Covered _____

Comments: _____

_____

_____

_____

Type of Policy _____

Name of Insurance Company _____ Policy No. _____

Agent's Name _____ Phone No. _____

Address _____

City _____ State _____ Zip _____

Issue Date _____ Expiration Date _____

Premiums Paid Annually _____ Monthly _____

Office to Which Premiums Are Paid _____

Benefits Provided _____ Policy Owner _____

Location of Policy _____

Persons Covered _____

Comments: _____

_____

_____

_____

Type of Policy _____

Name of Insurance Company _____ Policy No. _____

Agent's Name _____ Phone No. _____

Address _____

City _____ State _____ Zip _____

Issue Date _____ Expiration Date _____

Premiums Paid Annually _____ Monthly _____

Office to Which Premiums Are Paid _____

Benefits Provided _____ Policy Owner _____

Location of Policy _____

Persons Covered _____

Comments: _____

_____

_____

_____

Type of Policy _____

Name of Insurance Company _____ Policy No. _____

Agent's Name _____ Phone No. _____

Address _____

City _____ State _____ Zip _____

Issue Date _____ Expiration Date _____

Premiums Paid Annually _____ Monthly _____

Office to Which Premiums Are Paid _____

Benefits Provided _____ Policy Owner _____

Location of Policy _____

Persons Covered _____

Comments: _____

_____

_____

_____

Name of Insured _____

Name of Insurance Company _____

Agent's Name _____ Phone No. _____

Address _____ City _____ State _____

Type of Insurance _____ Policy No. _____

Issue Date _____ Expiration Date _____

Total Death Benefits _____ Cash Value _____

Beneficiary _____ Policy Owner _____

Premiums Paid Annually _____ Monthly _____

Office to Which Premiums Are Paid _____

Location of Policy _____

Name of Insured _____

Name of Insurance Company _____

Agent's Name _____ Phone No. _____

Address _____ City _____ State _____

Type of Insurance _____ Policy No. _____

Issue Date _____ Expiration Date _____

Total Death Benefits _____ Cash Value _____

Beneficiary _____ Policy Owner _____

Premiums Paid Annually _____ Monthly _____

Office to Which Premiums Are Paid _____

Location of Policy _____

Comments: _____

_____

_____

_____

_____

_____

_____

_____

Name of Insured _____

Name of Insurance Company _____

Agent's Name _____ Phone No. _____

Address _____ City _____ State _____

Type of Insurance _____ Policy No. _____

Issue Date _____ Expiration Date _____

Total Death Benefits _____ Cash Value _____

Beneficiary _____ Policy Owner _____

Premiums Paid Annually _____ Monthly _____

Office to Which Premiums Are Paid _____

Location of Policy _____

Name of Insured _____

Name of Insurance Company _____

Agent's Name _____ Phone No. _____

Address _____ City _____ State _____

Type of Insurance _____ Policy No. _____

Issue Date _____ Expiration Date _____

Total Death Benefits _____ Cash Value _____

Beneficiary _____ Policy Owner _____

Premiums Paid Annually _____ Monthly _____

Office to Which Premiums Are Paid _____

Location of Policy _____

Comments: _____

_____

_____

_____

_____

_____

_____

_____

Disability & Workman's Compensation

Illness or Injury _____

Name of Insurance Company _____ Policy No. _____

Agent's Name _____ Phone No. _____

Street Address _____ City _____ State _____

Benefits _____

Location of Policy _____

_____

_____

Unemployment Insurance _____

Monthly Benefits _____

_____

_____

_____

_____

Social Security _____

_____

_____

_____

_____

Other _____

_____

_____

_____

_____

_____

_____

_____

_____

_____

_____

_____

Disability & Workman's Compensation

Illness or Injury _____

Name of Insurance Company _____ *Policy No.* _____

Agent's Name _____ *Phone No.* _____

Street Address _____ *City* _____ *State* _____

Benefits _____

Location of Policy _____

_____

_____

Unemployment Insurance _____

Monthly Benefits _____

_____

_____

_____

_____

Social Security _____

_____

_____

_____

_____

Other _____

_____

_____

_____

_____

_____

_____

_____

_____

_____

_____

Property Insurance

Property Insured _____

Name of Insurance Company _____

Agent's Name _____ Phone No. _____

Street Address _____

City _____ State _____ Zip _____

Type of Insurance _____ Policy No. _____

Issue Date _____ Expiration Date _____

Total Coverage _____ Policy Owner _____

Premiums Paid Annually _____ Monthly _____

Office To Which Premiums Are Paid _____

Location of Policy _____

_____

_____

_____

_____

Property Insured _____

Name of Insurance Company _____

Agent's Name _____ Phone No. _____

Street Address _____

City _____ State _____ Zip _____

Type of Insurance _____ Policy No. _____

Issue Date _____ Expiration Date _____

Total Coverage _____ Policy Owner _____

Premiums Paid Annually _____ Monthly _____

Office To Which Premiums Are Paid _____

Location of Policy _____

_____

_____

_____

_____

Property Insurance

Property Insured _____

Name of Insurance Company _____

Agent's Name _____ Phone No. _____

Street Address _____

City _____ State _____ Zip _____

Type of Insurance _____ Policy No. _____

Issue Date _____ Expiration Date _____

Total Coverage _____ Policy Owner _____

Premiums Paid Annually _____ Monthly _____

Office To Which Premiums Are Paid _____

Location of Policy _____

_____

_____

_____

_____

Property Insured _____

Name of Insurance Company _____

Agent's Name _____ Phone No. _____

Street Address _____

City _____ State _____ Zip _____

Type of Insurance _____ Policy No. _____

Issue Date _____ Expiration Date _____

Total Coverage _____ Policy Owner _____

Premiums Paid Annually _____ Monthly _____

Office To Which Premiums Are Paid _____

Location of Policy _____

_____

_____

_____

_____

Automobile Insurance

Automobile Insured _____ Vehicle ID No. _____

Name of Insurance Company _____

Agent's Name _____ Phone No. _____

Street Address _____

City _____ State _____ Zip _____

Amount of Coverage _____ Policy No. _____

Date of Issue _____ Expiration Date _____ Renewal Date _____

Premiums Paid Annually _____ Monthly _____ Quarterly _____

Office To Which Premiums Are Paid _____

Location of Policy _____ Policy Owner _____

Automobile Insured _____ Vehicle ID No. _____

Name of Insurance Company _____

Agent's Name _____ Phone No. _____

Street Address _____

City _____ State _____ Zip _____

Amount of Coverage _____ Policy No. _____

Date of Issue _____ Expiration Date _____ Renewal Date _____

Premiums Paid Annually _____ Monthly _____ Quarterly _____

Office To Which Premiums Are Paid _____

Location of Policy _____ Policy Owner _____

_____

_____

_____

_____

_____

_____

_____

_____

_____

_____

Automobile Insurance

Automobile Insured _____ Vehicle ID No. _____

Name of Insurance Company _____

Agent's Name _____ Phone No. _____

Street Address _____

City _____ State _____ Zip _____

Amount of Coverage _____ Policy No. _____

Date of Issue _____ Expiration Date _____ Renewal Date _____

Premiums Paid Annually _____ Monthly _____ Quarterly _____

Office To Which Premiums Are Paid _____

Location of Policy _____ Policy Owner _____

Automobile Insured _____ Vehicle ID No. _____

Name of Insurance Company _____

Agent's Name _____ Phone No. _____

Street Address _____

City _____ State _____ Zip _____

Amount of Coverage _____ Policy No. _____

Date of Issue _____ Expiration Date _____ Renewal Date _____

Premiums Paid Annually _____ Monthly _____ Quarterly _____

Office To Which Premiums Are Paid _____

Location of Policy _____ Policy Owner _____

_____

_____

_____

_____

_____

_____

_____

_____

_____

Other Insurance

Jewelry • Furs • Marine • Credit • Water Damage • Dental

FLOATERS

Name of Insurance Company_____ Policy No._____

Agent's Name_____ Phone No._____

Street Address_____ City_____ State_____

Expiration Date_____ Premiums: Monthly_____ Quarterly_____ Annually_____

Location of Policy_____

Insured Items_____

_____

_____

Name of Insurance Company_____ Policy No._____

Agent's Name_____ Phone No._____

Street Address_____ City_____ State_____

Expiration Date_____ Premiums: Monthly_____ Quarterly_____ Annually_____

Location of Policy_____

Insured Items_____

_____

_____

Name of Insurance Company_____ Policy No._____

Agent's Name_____ Phone No._____

Street Address_____ City_____ State_____

Expiration Date_____ Premiums: Monthly_____ Quarterly_____ Annually_____

Location of Policy_____

Insured Items_____

_____

_____

Social Security

*T*he basic purpose of Social Security is to provide a continuing income to individuals and their families when normal paychecks stop or are reduced by retirement, disability, or death.

Social Security benefits include not only monthly retirement payments to the person covered, but for disability and death benefits to survivors, as well. Medicare benefits also are paid through the Social Security Administration.

Your Social Security tax is deducted from your wages each payday. Your employer matches your payment and sends the combined amount to the Internal Revenue Service.

Many of us are unaware that we can write the Social Security Administration and request a statement of the amount of earnings credited to your Social Security account. There is no charge for this service. Either call for the information at 1-800-234-5772, or send a postcard to:

Social Security Administration
Wilkes-Barre Data Operations Center
P.O. Box 20
Wilkes-Barre, PA 19703

Include your name, Social Security number, date of birth, address with zip code, and your signature. You may be pleasantly surprised to learn how much money has been credited to your account over the years.

To request a statement of your estimated future benefits, request Form SSA-7004-PC-OP1 from the above address or the nearest Social Security district office. (Check the U.S. Government pages of your telephone directory). You may also obtain a complete, up-to-date benefits pamphlet from your local Social Security office.

Once you realize how easy it is to attain this information, make periodic checks against your W-2 forms. Mistakes can be made, parti-cularly when you move from one job to another. Your earnings must be correctly reported if you are to receive your full benefit.

In the event of your death, certain vital papers will be required from your family for making an official claim. To save unnecessary delay all papers should be together, and your family should know where they are kept. The claimant will need your Social Security card, proof of birth, proof of marriage, proof of birth of your spouse and each child, military discharge papers (if issued after September 16, 1940), and your W-2 or other proof of wages for the previous year. All claims must be accompanied by a death certificate.

There are two types of death benefits: a "lump-sum" benefit designed to help cover funeral expenses; or 2) a monthly income paid to dependents and eligible survivors. Benefit payments are determined by worker's average income and age of surviving dependents.

Claims also can be filed by writing to the Social Security office, giving the name and Social Security number of the deceased. The office will return claim forms with instructions for completing them.

All those paying into the Social Security program are building lifetime protection for themselves and their families. Social Security payments are not intended to replace all lost earnings. Many people are supplementing Social Security payments with savings, pensions, investments, other insurance, and/or part time employment. (Retired workers between the ages of 65 and 69 may earn an additional $9,360 before suffering a loss of benefits. Individuals 70 years of age or older may earn any amount without incurring benefit loss).

Personal Property Photo Record

Everyone has special possessions that have an important place in the family's history. They may be items of monetary value, such as jewelry, silverware or china; or items of essentially sentimental significance: your grandmother's wedding dress, old family photographs, or the family Bible, for example. All of these precious possessions should be inventoried so that your family will know they exist and where they can be found. In compiling such an inventory you may be surprised to turn up long forgotten family treasures.

Keeping an account of these treasured objects is a major responsibility because as you inherited them, so you will pass them on to future generations. And what you have acquired in your own lifetime will in turn become the heirlooms of the future. You may have formed an especially notable art or old books collection. Some of your house or apartment furnishings will doubtless enrich the family holdings. Any hobby equipment of value, such as cameras or tools, may also become part of your legacy to the family.

When making your will, you should carefully consider passing on your prized possessions to those who will have the greatest appreciation and respect for them and who will care for and preserve these family heirlooms in their own lifetimes for the next generation.

Keep a record of all valuables, including serial numbers, so that in case of theft an immediate and complete reporting can be made to the police.

Most of us underestimate the value our possessions will have for our descendents.

Moreover, we tend to take these objects for granted simply because we live with them. But unless they are carefully itemized and, if necessary, insured, they cannot be properly protected. And if any of these possessions are insured against loss, theft, or damage, a photographic record is essential for identification purposes. The following pages are designed to accommodate such a record. After making your inventory, take photographs of the valuable items and paste them in. Should you have a fire or be robbed, these pictures will be useful to the police and facilitate insurance claims.

The houses or apartments in which you and your family have lived are as much a part of your history as are the objects within—"if only the walls could talk," as the old saying goes. And every move your family has made—whether to a nearby location or to a distant city—marks a significant change in your life circumstances. Pages are therefore included on which to record the addresses of all the places you have lived, along with any special recollections you may have. And if there is real estate that you have inherited or that otherwise belongs in the family, this too should be entered into the ledger.

Increase your chances of recovering stolen property by inscribing codes or serial numbers in some inconspicuous place on all valuable objects. In the event of theft, report immediately all information to your local police. The FBI has established a new computerized National Crime Information Center which uses that information for important fast checks of fences.

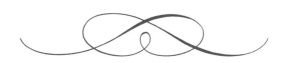

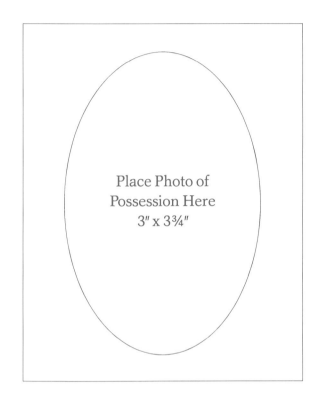

Item Description_____

Date_____

Serial No._____

Origin_____

_____

Estimated Value_____

Comments:_____

_____

_____

_____

_____

_____

_____

_____

_____

_____

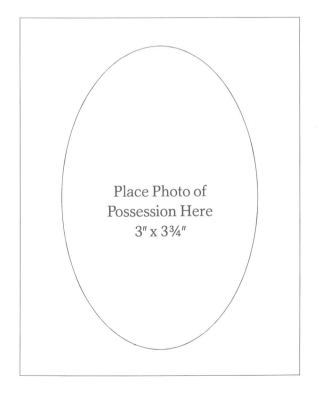

Item Description_____

Date_____

Serial No._____

Origin_____

_____

Estimated Value_____

Comments:_____

_____

_____

_____

_____

_____

_____

_____

_____

_____

_____

Personal Property

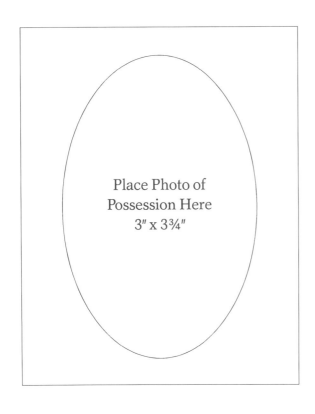

Place Photo of
Possession Here
3″ x 3¾″

Item Description _____

Date _____

Serial No. _____

Origin _____

_____

Estimated Value _____

Comments: _____

_____

_____

_____

_____

_____

_____

_____

_____

_____

_____

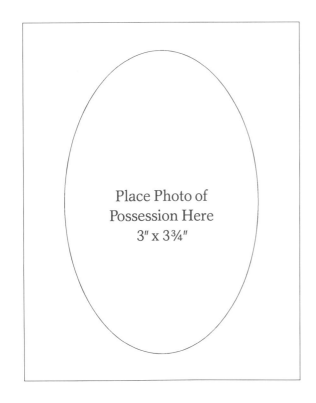

Place Photo of
Possession Here
3″ x 3¾″

Item Description _____

Date _____

Serial No. _____

Origin _____

_____

Estimated Value _____

Comments: _____

_____

_____

_____

_____

_____

_____

_____

_____

_____

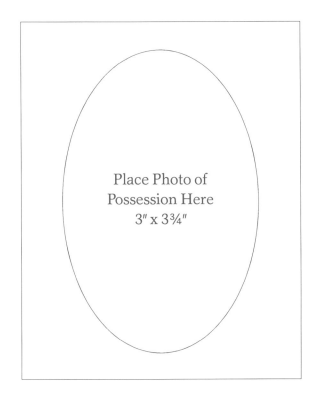

Place Photo of
Possession Here
3″ x 3¾″

Item Description _____

Date _____

Serial No. _____

Origin _____

_____

Estimated Value _____

Comments: _____

_____

_____

_____

_____

_____

_____

_____

_____

_____

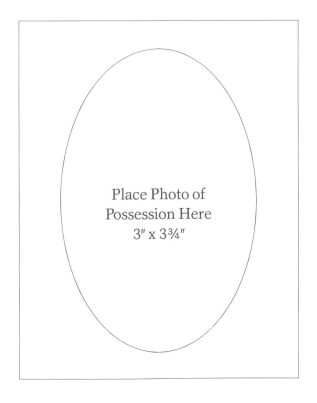

Place Photo of
Possession Here
3″ x 3¾″

Item Description _____

Date _____

Serial No. _____

Origin _____

_____

Estimated Value _____

Comments: _____

_____

_____

_____

_____

_____

_____

_____

_____

_____

Personal Property

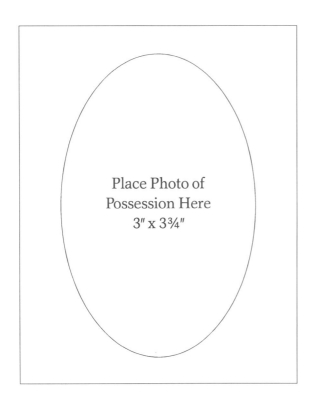

Place Photo of
Possession Here
3" x 3¾"

Item Description _____

Date _____

Serial No. _____

Origin _____

_____

Estimated Value _____

Comments: _____

_____

_____

_____

_____

_____

_____

_____

_____

_____

_____

_____

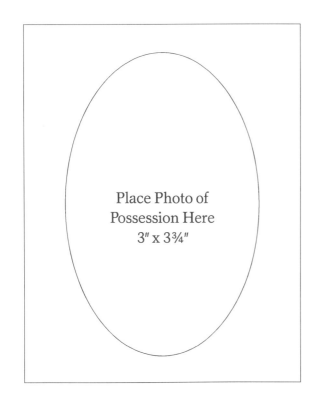

Place Photo of
Possession Here
3" x 3¾"

Item Description _____

Date _____

Serial No. _____

Origin _____

_____

Estimated Value _____

Comments: _____

_____

_____

_____

_____

_____

_____

_____

_____

_____

_____

_____

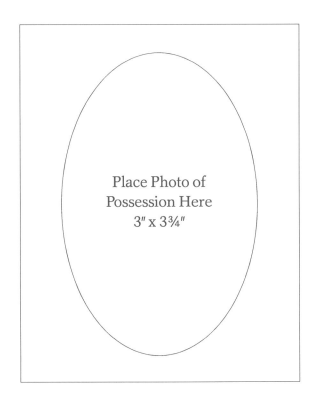

Item Description _____

Date _____

Serial No. _____

Origin _____

_____

Estimated Value _____

Comments: _____

_____

_____

_____

_____

_____

_____

_____

_____

_____

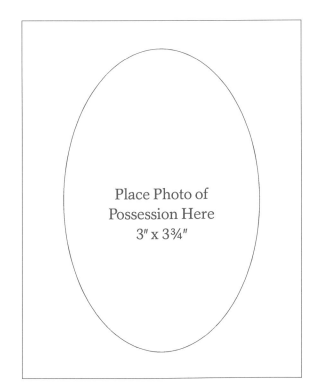

Item Description _____

Date _____

Serial No. _____

Origin _____

_____

Estimated Value _____

Comments: _____

_____

_____

_____

_____

_____

_____

_____

_____

_____

Personal Property

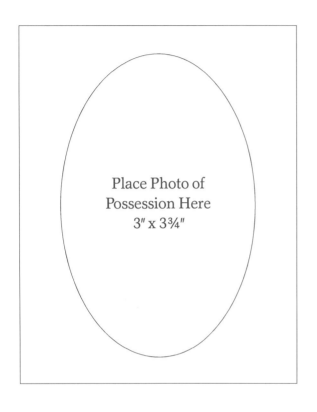

Place Photo of
Possession Here
3" x 3¾"

Item Description _____

Date _____

Serial No. _____

Origin _____

_____

Estimated Value _____

Comments: _____

_____

_____

_____

_____

_____

_____

_____

_____

_____

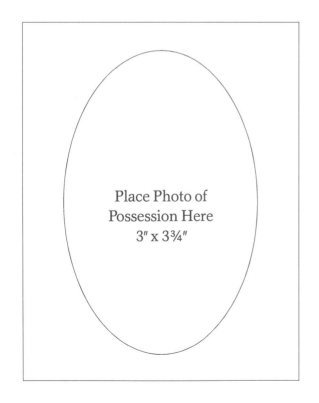

Place Photo of
Possession Here
3" x 3¾"

Item Description _____

Date _____

Serial No. _____

Origin _____

_____

Estimated Value _____

Comments: _____

_____

_____

_____

_____

_____

_____

_____

_____

_____

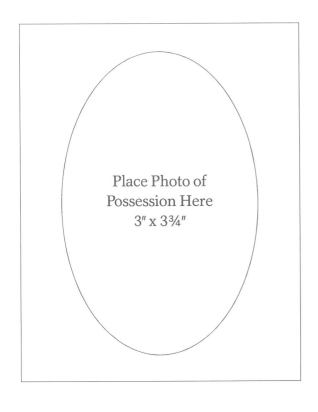

Place Photo of
Possession Here
3" x 3¾"

Item Description _____

Date _____

Serial No. _____

Origin _____

_____

Estimated Value _____

Comments: _____

_____

_____

_____

_____

_____

_____

_____

_____

_____

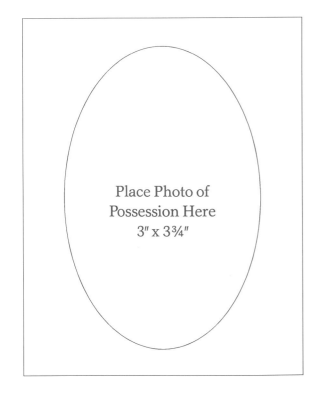

Place Photo of
Possession Here
3" x 3¾"

Item Description _____

Date _____

Serial No. _____

Origin _____

_____

Estimated Value _____

Comments: _____

_____

_____

_____

_____

_____

_____

_____

_____

_____

Personal Property

Collections · Stamps · Coins · Paintings · Guns · Antiques · etc.

Item	Estimated Value	Location	Comments	Date

Personal Property

Collections · Stamps · Coins · Paintings · Guns · Antiques · etc.

Item	Estimated Value	Location	Comments	Date

Our Homes (Dates & Addresses)

Street Address _____

City _____ State _____

Resided From _____ to _____

Neighbors _____

Comments _____

_____

Street Address _____

City _____ State _____

Resided From _____ to _____

Neighbors _____

Comments _____

_____

Street Address _____

City _____ State _____

Resided From _____ to _____

Neighbors _____

Comments _____

_____

Street Address _____

City _____ State _____

Resided From _____ to _____

Neighbors _____

Comments _____

_____

Street Address _____

City _____ State _____

Resided From _____ to _____

Neighbors _____

Comments _____

_____

Our Homes (Dates & Addresses)

Street Address _____

City _____ State _____

Resided From _____ to _____

Neighbors _____

Comments _____

_____

Street Address _____

City _____ State _____

Resided From _____ to _____

Neighbors _____

Comments _____

_____

Street Address _____

City _____ State _____

Resided From _____ to _____

Neighbors _____

Comments _____

_____

Street Address _____

City _____ State _____

Resided From _____ to _____

Neighbors _____

Comments _____

_____

Street Address _____

City _____ State _____

Resided From _____ to _____

Neighbors _____

Comments _____

_____

Other Real Estate

Location_____ Date_____

City_____ State_____

Description_____

Valued At:_____ Owned Since: Year_____

Comments_____

Location_____ Date_____

City_____ State_____

Description_____

Valued At:_____ Owned Since: Year_____

Comments_____

Location_____ Date_____

City_____ State_____

Description_____

Valued At:_____ Owned Since: Year_____

Comments_____

Location_____ Date_____

City_____ State_____

Description_____

Valued At:_____ Owned Since: Year_____

Comments_____

Location_____ Date_____

City_____ State_____

Description_____

Valued At:_____ Owned Since: Year_____

Comments_____

Real Estate Improvements

Alterations · Energy Conservation · New Roofing · New Windows
Air Conditioning · Tree/Shrubs · Driveway · New Doors
Storms/Screens · Porch · etc.

SAVE ALL BILLS

Location_____ Date_____

Improvements_____ Cost_____

Contractor_____ Telephone No. _____

_____

_____

Location_____ Date_____

Improvements_____ Cost_____

Contractor_____ Telephone No. _____

_____

_____

Location_____ Date_____

Improvements_____ Cost_____

Contractor_____ Telephone No. _____

_____

_____

Location_____ Date_____

Improvements_____ Cost_____

Contractor_____ Telephone No. _____

_____

_____

Real Estate Improvements

Alterations • Energy Conservation • New Roofing • New Windows
Air Conditioning • Tree/Shrubs • Driveway • New Doors
Storms/Screens • Porch • etc.

SAVE ALL BILLS

Location _____ Date _____

Improvements _____ Cost _____

_____

Contractor _____ Telephone No. _____

_____

_____

Location _____ Date _____

Improvements _____ Cost _____

_____

Contractor _____ Telephone No. _____

_____

_____

Location _____ Date _____

Improvements _____ Cost _____

_____

Contractor _____ Telephone No. _____

_____

_____

Location _____ Date _____

Improvements _____ Cost _____

_____

Contractor _____ Telephone No. _____

_____

_____

Location_____ Date_____

City_____ State_____

Description _____

Valued At:_____ Owned Since: Year_____

Comments _____

_____

Location_____ Date_____

City_____ State_____

Description _____

Valued At:_____ Owned Since: Year_____

Comments _____

_____

Location_____ Date_____

City_____ State_____

Description _____

Valued At:_____ Owned Since: Year_____

Comments _____

_____

Location_____ Date_____

City_____ State_____

Description _____

Valued At:_____ Owned Since: Year_____

Comments _____

_____

Location_____ Date_____

City_____ State_____

Description _____

Valued At:_____ Owned Since: Year_____

Comments _____

_____

Business & Employment

*E*ven though earning a living occupies a good portion of our days, it is the part of our lives least known to other family members. Your spouse or children may seem to be familiar with your work because you speak about it — about encounters with colleagues, the success or failure of a project, plans for the future, and the like. But as interesting as such information is, it will neither prepare your family to settle your business affairs properly, nor assure that they know their rights. Whether you are self-employed or work for others, your family must have access to some basic facts that explain your legal status within the business and its obligations, if any, to your heirs.

As a general rule when you accept employment you have entered into a contract which specifies work to be done for a specific wage for a certain number of hours. Work contracts are usually not in writing but are protected by law as if they were. In situations when contracts are signed, both you and the employer can be held to it.

By law, employers are required to have Workers' Compensation Insurance. Some states have laws that require employers to insure their employees against illness or injury which is not job-related. Employers must also contribute to Social Security and pay for unemployment insurance.

Do the health insurance plans to which you belong cease at your death or will coverage for your family be maintained? Some companies automatically provide life insurance policies for certain employees. If you are so insured, your family should know the amount of the policy and the identity of the beneficiaries. As for retirement income, you have probably enrolled in some kind of plan through a company or as an individual. But there is such a variety of plans available, and each plan with a variety of options, that your heirs will need to know the answers to a few important questions: if you do not live to retirement age, can they collect all or part of your pension, and in a lump sum or through periodic payments? If you are already retired, check your pension program to see what plan you opted for. With some plans, you receive maximum monthly payments which cease at death; with others, the payments during your lifetime are smaller, but the annuity will continue to be paid to your beneficiaries. The personnel benefits officer in your company or your own insurance agent can help answer these questions and evaluate your present plan in terms of your family's needs.

Are you part of a profit-sharing program? Are the shares in your possession or does the company have them? Above all, let your family know how many shares or what percentage of the profits you receive per year and whether they are entitled to inherit your holdings. If you own a business yourself, or jointly with one or more partners, your family must be apprised of your contractual agreements. Matters that you take for granted about the structure of the business — exactly how much of it you own, what your obligations are to others — will be difficult for your family to disentangle without you. A lawyer, of course, can handle these affairs, but your heirs should nevertheless know what is due them.

Don't leave the responsibility for telling the family about your business affairs in the hands of partners or co-workers. Although these people may be knowledgeable and well-intentioned, their concern for your family can never be greater than yours. The information you provide will be your family's best protection.

In the event of a crisis, a company personnel benefits officer can provide all the necessary information that may be needed.

Employment Data

Name _____

Employer _____ Starting Date _____

Address _____ State _____ Zip _____

Nature of Business _____ Telephone No. _____

Immediate Supervisor and Title _____

Your Title _____

Your Responsibilities _____

Benefit Plans: Life Insurance ☐ Blue Cross ☐ Blue Shield ☐ Dental ☐ Disability

☐ Major Medical ☐ Pension Plan ☐ Profit Sharing ☐ Prescriptions

☐ Accident Insurance ☐ Stock Options ☐ Other _____

_____

Location of Benefit Plan Booklets _____

Union Name _____ Telephone No. _____

Benefits _____

Date of Departure _____ Reason of Leaving _____

Achievements and/or Comments: _____

_____

_____

_____

_____

_____

Other Jobs: _____

_____

_____

_____

_____

_____

_____

_____

_____

_____

Employment Data

Name _____

Employer _____ Starting Date _____

Address _____ State _____ Zip _____

Nature of Business _____ Telephone No. _____

Immediate Supervisor and Title _____

Your Title _____

Your Responsibilities _____

Benefit Plans: Life Insurance ☐ Blue Cross ☐ Blue Shield ☐ Dental ☐ Disability

☐ Major Medical ☐ Pension Plan ☐ Profit Sharing ☐ Prescriptions

☐ Accident Insurance ☐ Stock Options ☐ Other _____

Location of Benefit Plan Booklets _____

Union Name _____ Telephone No. _____

Benefits _____

Date of Departure _____ Reason of Leaving _____

Achievements and/or Comments: _____

_____

_____

_____

_____

Other Jobs: _____

_____

_____

_____

_____

_____

_____

_____

_____

_____

Employment Data

Name _____

Employer _____ Starting Date _____

Address _____ State _____ Zip _____

Nature of Business _____ Telephone No. _____

Immediate Supervisor and Title _____

Your Title _____

Your Responsibilities _____

Benefit Plans: Life Insurance ☐ Blue Cross ☐ Blue Shield ☐ Dental ☐ Disability

☐ Major Medical ☐ Pension Plan ☐ Profit Sharing ☐ Prescriptions

☐ Accident Insurance ☐ Stock Options ☐ Other _____

_____

Location of Benefit Plan Booklets _____

Union Name _____ Telephone No. _____

Benefits _____

Date of Departure _____ Reason of Leaving _____

Achievements and/or Comments: _____

_____

_____

_____

_____

_____

Other Jobs: _____

_____

_____

_____

_____

_____

_____

_____

_____

Employment Data

Name _____

Employer _____ Starting Date _____

Address _____ State _____ Zip _____

Nature of Business _____ Telephone No. _____

Immediate Supervisor and Title _____

Your Title _____

Your Responsibilities _____

Benefit Plans: Life Insurance ☐ Blue Cross ☐ Blue Shield ☐ Dental ☐ Disability

☐ Major Medical ☐ Pension Plan ☐ Profit Sharing ☐ Prescriptions

☐ Accident Insurance ☐ Stock Options ☐ Other _____

_____

Location of Benefit Plan Booklets _____

Union Name _____ Telephone No. _____

Benefits _____

Date of Departure _____ Reason of Leaving _____

Achievements and/or Comments: _____

_____

_____

_____

_____

Other Jobs: _____

_____

_____

_____

_____

_____

_____

_____

_____

Employment Data

Name _____

Employer _____ Starting Date _____

Address _____ State _____ Zip _____

Nature of Business _____ Telephone No. _____

Immediate Supervisor and Title _____

Your Title _____

Your Responsibilities _____

Benefit Plans: Life Insurance ☐ Blue Cross ☐ Blue Shield ☐ Dental ☐ Disability

☐ Major Medical ☐ Pension Plan ☐ Profit Sharing ☐ Prescriptions

☐ Accident Insurance ☐ Stock Options ☐ Other _____

Location of Benefit Plan Booklets _____

Union Name _____ Telephone No. _____

Benefits _____

Date of Departure _____ Reason of Leaving _____

Achievements and/or Comments: _____

_____

_____

_____

_____

_____

Other Jobs: _____

_____

_____

_____

_____

_____

_____

_____

_____

_____

Business Affiliations

Name of Business _____ Date _____

Address _____ City _____ State _____

Type of Business _____ Ownership Percentage _____

Location of Stock Certificates: _____

Location of Survivors' Agreement _____

Location of Other Agreements: Partnerships, Options, Company Papers, etc. _____

Trusted Advisor: Name _____ Telephone _____

           Address _____ City _____ State _____

Accountant: Name _____ Telephone _____

           Address _____ City _____ State _____

Other Stockholders and Interest % _____

_____

_____

_____

Name of Business _____ Date _____

Address _____ City _____ State _____

Type of Business _____ Ownership Percentage _____

Location of Stock Certificates: _____

Location of Survivors' Agreement _____

Location of Other Agreements: Partnerships, Options, Company Papers, etc. _____

Trusted Advisor: Name _____ Telephone _____

           Address _____ City _____ State _____

Accountant: Name _____ Telephone _____

           Address _____ City _____ State _____

Other Stockholders and Interest % _____

_____

_____

_____

Business Affiliations

Name of Business _____ Date _____

Address _____ City _____ State _____

Type of Business _____ Ownership Percentage _____

Location of Stock Certificates: _____

Location of Survivors' Agreement _____

Location of Other Agreements: Partnerships, Options, Company Papers, etc. _____

Trusted Advisor: Name _____ Telephone _____

        Address _____ City _____ State _____

Accountant: Name _____ Telephone _____

        Address _____ City _____ State _____

Other Stockholders and Interest % _____

_____

_____

_____

Name of Business _____ Date _____

Address _____ City _____ State _____

Type of Business _____ Ownership Percentage _____

Location of Stock Certificates: _____

Location of Survivors' Agreement _____

Location of Other Agreements: Partnerships, Options, Company Papers, etc. _____

Trusted Advisor: Name _____ Telephone _____

        Address _____ City _____ State _____

Accountant: Name _____ Telephone _____

        Address _____ City _____ State _____

Other Stockholders and Interest % _____

_____

_____

_____

Business Affiliations

Name of Business _____ Date _____

Address _____ City _____ State _____

Type of Business _____ Ownership Percentage _____

Location of Stock Certificates: _____

Location of Survivors' Agreement _____

Location of Other Agreements: Partnerships, Options, Company Papers, etc. _____

Trusted Advisor: Name _____ Telephone _____

    Address _____ City _____ State _____

Accountant: Name _____ Telephone _____

    Address _____ City _____ State _____

Other Stockholders and Interest % _____

_____

_____

_____

Name of Business _____ Date _____

Address _____ City _____ State _____

Type of Business _____ Ownership Percentage _____

Location of Stock Certificates: _____

Location of Survivors' Agreement _____

Location of Other Agreements: Partnerships, Options, Company Papers, etc. _____

Trusted Advisor: Name _____ Telephone _____

    Address _____ City _____ State _____

Accountant: Name _____ Telephone _____

    Address _____ City _____ State _____

Other Stockholders and Interest % _____

_____

_____

_____

Business Affiliations

Name of Business _____ Date _____

Address _____ City _____ State _____

Type of Business _____ Ownership Percentage _____

Location of Stock Certificates: _____

Location of Survivors' Agreement _____

Location of Other Agreements: Partnerships, Options, Company Papers, etc. _____

Trusted Advisor: Name _____ Telephone _____

             Address _____ City _____ State _____

Accountant: Name _____ Telephone _____

             Address _____ City _____ State _____

Other Stockholders and Interest % _____

_____

_____

_____

Name of Business _____ Date _____

Address _____ City _____ State _____

Type of Business _____ Ownership Percentage _____

Location of Stock Certificates: _____

Location of Survivors' Agreement _____

Location of Other Agreements: Partnerships, Options, Company Papers, etc. _____

Trusted Advisor: Name _____ Telephone _____

             Address _____ City _____ State _____

Accountant: Name _____ Telephone _____

             Address _____ City _____ State _____

Other Stockholders and Interest % _____

_____

_____

_____

Group Retirement Plan

Name of Employer _____ Date _____

Address _____ City _____ State _____

Nature of Business _____ Telephone No. _____

Type of Plan _____ Plan No. _____ Employer I.D. No. _____

Amount Vested _____ Plan Administrator _____

Name _____

Address _____

City _____ State _____

Type of Administration _____ Telephone No. _____

Trustees _____

_____

Benefits _____ Location of Information _____

_____

_____

_____

Name of Employer _____ Date _____

Address _____ City _____ State _____

Nature of Business _____ Telephone No. _____

Type of Plan _____ Plan No. _____ Employer I.D. No. _____

Amount Vested _____ Plan Administrator _____

Name _____

Address _____

City _____ State _____

Type of Administration _____ Telephone No. _____

Trustees _____

_____

Benefits _____ Location of Information _____

_____

_____

_____

Retirement Income

Monthly Income

Social Security

IRA (Individual Retirement Account)

Keogh

Company Pension Plan

Annuities

Investments

Other

Family Finances

An exact account of your assets and liabilities will give you an accurate measure of your net worth. For yourself, such an overview is essential for annual budgeting, taxation estimates, investment and estate planning. It is also essential when emergencies arise to know what financial sources can be tapped. But for your family, the details you provide in the following pages may be even more vital. Although many people tend to keep their financial affairs private, some written statement should be available to your loved ones at your death, if not before. Only in this way can they be assured of financial security, assured that they need not rush into decisions at a trying moment. With certain knowledge of your financial holdings, they can re-plan their lives with confidence, remaining in control of their future, without having to trust to memory or put their welfare in the hands of others.

Your financial assets may be extremely varied, ranging from a local savings account to complicated holdings in investment companies. Distinguish between those which generate current income through interest or dividends, those holdings (stocks, bonds, commodities) traded for capital gains, and those which secure the future in the form of annuities, trust funds, and the like. And any recommendations you make will be invaluable. As the person responsible for financial matters and, at the same time, most concerned for your loved ones, you may have the best ideas about whether, for instance, to sell securities and reinvest the capital or keep them for the income they produce.

A breakdown of your assets will also help you advise your family about how to meet on-going expenses. For the same reason, you should compile a list of the fixed bills that come in regularly. This will enable your family to better estimate monthly expenses and plan accordingly. In addition, indicate which of your assets are owned jointly or for which various funds or policies you have designated beneficiaries.

Does any person or organization owe you money? Even if you made a personal loan to a friend, it should be recorded, along with the terms of the agreement and schedule of payments. And remember to note down the location of all papers, certificates, etc.—they will most likely be in your safe-deposit box.

Whatever liabilities you have incurred will affect your family's financial future as much as will your assets. Your debts may be in the form of mortgages, bank loans, liens on salary or property, or personal obligations. Again, the terms and payment schedules should be carefully outlined and the pertinent documents identified and located. Don't forget that some debts are cancelled at death and others covered by debt insurance. Those that remain—those that your heirs will have to assume—form an integral part of your estate.

Remember that all good record keeping is simply keeping current all the right information and papers in the right place, and discarding everything that is obsolete, that which serves no purpose.

Items that should be kept in a home file:
Canceled checks and bank statements
State and federal income tax returns
Insurance, retirement and pension plans
Paycheck stubs
Credit card numbers & telephone numbers
Social Security cards
Warranties
Burial instructions

Bank Accounts—Financial Assets

Bank Name _____ Telephone No. _____

Address _____ City _____ State _____

Type of Account: Savings ☐ Checking ☐ Account No. _____

Account Is In the Name Of: _____

Savings Account Books Are Located At: _____

Authorized Names Who Can Deposit and Withdraw Monies: _____

Authorized Names Who Can Sign Checks: _____

Date Opened _____ Date Closed _____

_____

_____

Bank Name _____ Telephone No. _____

Address _____ City _____ State _____

Type of Account: Savings ☐ Checking ☐ Account No. _____

Account Is In the Name Of: _____

Savings Account Books Are Located At: _____

Authorized Names Who Can Deposit and Withdraw Monies: _____

Authorized Names Who Can Sign Checks: _____

Date Opened _____ Date Closed _____

_____

_____

Bank Name _____ Telephone No. _____

Address _____ City _____ State _____

Type of Account: Savings ☐ Checking ☐ Account No. _____

Account Is In the Name Of: _____

Savings Account Books Are Located At: _____

Authorized Names Who Can Deposit and Withdraw Monies: _____

Authorized Names Who Can Sign Checks: _____

Date Opened _____ Date Closed _____

_____

_____

Bank Accounts—Financial Assets

Bank Name _____ Telephone No. _____

Address _____ City _____ State _____

Type of Account: Savings ☐ Checking ☐ Account No. _____

Account Is In the Name Of: _____

Savings Account Books Are Located At: _____

Authorized Names Who Can Deposit and Withdraw Monies: _____

Authorized Names Who Can Sign Checks: _____

Date Opened _____ Date Closed _____

_____

_____

Bank Name _____ Telephone No. _____

Address _____ City _____ State _____

Type of Account: Savings ☐ Checking ☐ Account No. _____

Account Is In the Name Of: _____

Savings Account Books Are Located At: _____

Authorized Names Who Can Deposit and Withdraw Monies: _____

Authorized Names Who Can Sign Checks: _____

Date Opened _____ Date Closed _____

_____

_____

Bank Name _____ Telephone No. _____

Address _____ City _____ State _____

Type of Account: Savings ☐ Checking ☐ Account No. _____

Account Is In the Name Of: _____

Savings Account Books Are Located At: _____

Authorized Names Who Can Deposit and Withdraw Monies: _____

Authorized Names Who Can Sign Checks: _____

Date Opened _____ Date Closed _____

_____

_____

Bank Accounts—Financial Assets

Bank Name_____ Telephone No. _____

Address_____ City_____ State_____

Type of Account: Savings ☐ Checking ☐ Account No._____

Account Is In the Name Of: _____

Savings Account Books Are Located At: _____

Authorized Names Who Can Deposit and Withdraw Monies:_____

Authorized Names Who Can Sign Checks: _____

Date Opened_____ Date Closed_____

_____

_____

Bank Name_____ Telephone No. _____

Address_____ City_____ State_____

Type of Account: Savings ☐ Checking ☐ Account No._____

Account Is In the Name Of: _____

Savings Account Books Are Located At: _____

Authorized Names Who Can Deposit and Withdraw Monies:_____

Authorized Names Who Can Sign Checks: _____

Date Opened_____ Date Closed_____

_____

_____

Bank Name_____ Telephone No. _____

Address_____ City_____ State_____

Type of Account: Savings ☐ Checking ☐ Account No._____

Account Is In the Name Of: _____

Savings Account Books Are Located At: _____

Authorized Names Who Can Deposit and Withdraw Monies:_____

Authorized Names Who Can Sign Checks: _____

Date Opened_____ Date Closed_____

_____

_____

Credit Union Shares

Credit Union _____ Telephone No. _____

Address _____ City _____ State _____

Type of Account _____ Account No. _____

Account Is In the Name Of: _____

Comments _____

_____

_____

Credit Union _____ Telephone No. _____

Address _____ City _____ State _____

Type of Account _____ Account No. _____

Account Is In the Name Of: _____

Comments _____

_____

_____

Credit Union _____ Telephone No. _____

Address _____ City _____ State _____

Type of Account _____ Account No. _____

Account Is In the Name Of: _____

Comments _____

_____

_____

Credit Union _____ Telephone No. _____

Address _____ City _____ State _____

Type of Account _____ Account No. _____

Account Is In the Name Of: _____

Comments _____

_____

_____

Certificates of Deposit

Bank Name _____ Date _____

Address _____ City _____ State _____

Certificate No. _____ Amount Deposited $ _____ Date _____

Interest Rate _____ Date of Maturity _____ Location _____

Comments _____
_____
_____

Bank Name _____ Date _____

Address _____ City _____ State _____

Certificate No. _____ Amount Deposited $ _____ Date _____

Interest Rate _____ Date of Maturity _____ Location _____

Comments _____
_____
_____

Bank Name _____ Date _____

Address _____ City _____ State _____

Certificate No. _____ Amount Deposited $ _____ Date _____

Interest Rate _____ Date of Maturity _____ Location _____

Comments _____
_____
_____

Bank Name _____ Date _____

Address _____ City _____ State _____

Certificate No. _____ Amount Deposited $ _____ Date _____

Interest Rate _____ Date of Maturity _____ Location _____

Comments _____
_____
_____

Certificates of Deposit

Bank Name _____ Date _____

Address _____ City _____ State _____

Certificate No. _____ Amount Deposited $ _____ Date _____

Interest Rate _____ Date of Maturity _____ Location _____

Comments _____

_____

_____

Bank Name _____ Date _____

Address _____ City _____ State _____

Certificate No. _____ Amount Deposited $ _____ Date _____

Interest Rate _____ Date of Maturity _____ Location _____

Comments _____

_____

_____

Bank Name _____ Date _____

Address _____ City _____ State _____

Certificate No. _____ Amount Deposited $ _____ Date _____

Interest Rate _____ Date of Maturity _____ Location _____

Comments _____

_____

_____

Bank Name _____ Date _____

Address _____ City _____ State _____

Certificate No. _____ Amount Deposited $ _____ Date _____

Interest Rate _____ Date of Maturity _____ Location _____

Comments _____

_____

_____

Securities

Brokerage Firm _____ Telephone _____
Account Agent _____
Address _____ City _____ State _____
Account Is In The Name Of: _____ Account No. _____
Stock Name _____ Number of Shares _____ Unit Price _____
Transaction Date _____ Shares Bought At _____ Shares Sold At _____
Comments _____ Location of Certificate _____
_____
_____
_____

Brokerage Firm _____ Telephone _____
Account Agent _____
Address _____ City _____ State _____
Account Is In The Name Of: _____ Account No. _____
Stock Name _____ Number of Shares _____ Unit Price _____
Transaction Date _____ Shares Bought At _____ Shares Sold At _____
Comments _____ Location of Certificate _____
_____
_____
_____

Brokerage Firm _____ Telephone _____
Account Agent _____
Address _____ City _____ State _____
Account Is In The Name Of: _____ Account No. _____
Stock Name _____ Number of Shares _____ Unit Price _____
Transaction Date _____ Shares Bought At _____ Shares Sold At _____
Comments _____ Location of Certificate _____
_____
_____
_____

Securities

Brokerage Firm_____ Telephone _____

Account Agent_____

Address_____ City_____State_____

Account Is In The Name Of: _____ Account No._____

Stock Name_____ Number of Shares_____ Unit Price_____

Transaction Date_____ Shares Bought At_____ Shares Sold At_____

Comments _____ Location of Certificate_____

_____

_____

Brokerage Firm_____ Telephone _____

Account Agent_____

Address_____ City_____State_____

Account Is In The Name Of: _____ Account No._____

Stock Name_____ Number of Shares_____ Unit Price_____

Transaction Date_____ Shares Bought At_____ Shares Sold At_____

Comments _____ Location of Certificate_____

_____

_____

Brokerage Firm_____ Telephone _____

Account Agent_____

Address_____ City_____State_____

Account Is In The Name Of: _____ Account No._____

Stock Name_____ Number of Shares_____ Unit Price_____

Transaction Date_____ Shares Bought At_____ Shares Sold At_____

Comments _____ Location of Certificate_____

_____

_____

_____

Brokerage Firm_____ Telephone_____

Account Agent_____

Address_____ City_____ State_____

Account Is In The Name Of:_____ Account No._____

Stock Name_____ Number of Shares_____ Unit Price_____

Transaction Date_____ Shares Bought At_____ Shares Sold At_____

Comments_____ Location of Certificate_____

_____

_____

_____

Brokerage Firm_____ Telephone_____

Account Agent_____

Address_____ City_____ State_____

Account Is In The Name Of:_____ Account No._____

Stock Name_____ Number of Shares_____ Unit Price_____

Transaction Date_____ Shares Bought At_____ Shares Sold At_____

Comments_____ Location of Certificate_____

_____

_____

_____

Brokerage Firm_____ Telephone_____

Account Agent_____

Address_____ City_____ State_____

Account Is In The Name Of:_____ Account No._____

Stock Name_____ Number of Shares_____ Unit Price_____

Transaction Date_____ Shares Bought At_____ Shares Sold At_____

Comments_____ Location of Certificate_____

_____

_____

_____

_____

Commodities

Broker _____ Telephone _____

Address _____ City _____ State _____

Account Is In The Name Of: _____ Account No. _____

Name of Commodity _____ Amount Purchased _____ Purchase Price $ _____

Transaction Date _____ Bought At $ _____ Sold At $ _____

Location of Certificates _____ Comments _____

Broker _____ Telephone _____

Address _____ City _____ State _____

Account Is In The Name Of: _____ Account No. _____

Name of Commodity _____ Amount Purchased _____ Purchase Price $ _____

Transaction Date _____ Bought At $ _____ Sold At $ _____

Location of Certificates _____ Comments _____

Broker _____ Telephone _____

Address _____ City _____ State _____

Account Is In The Name Of: _____ Account No. _____

Name of Commodity _____ Amount Purchased _____ Purchase Price $ _____

Transaction Date _____ Bought At $ _____ Sold At $ _____

Location of Certificates _____ Comments _____

Broker _____ Telephone _____

Address _____ City _____ State _____

Account Is In The Name Of: _____ Account No. _____

Name of Commodity _____ Amount Purchased _____ Purchase Price $ _____

Transaction Date _____ Bought At $ _____ Sold At $ _____

Location of Certificates _____ Comments _____

Commodities

Broker _____ Telephone _____

Address _____ City _____ State _____

Account Is In The Name Of: _____ Account No. _____

Name of Commodity _____ Amount Purchased _____ Purchase Price $ _____

Transaction Date _____ Bought At $ _____ Sold At $ _____

Location of Certificates _____ Comments _____

Broker _____ Telephone _____

Address _____ City _____ State _____

Account Is In The Name Of: _____ Account No. _____

Name of Commodity _____ Amount Purchased _____ Purchase Price $ _____

Transaction Date _____ Bought At $ _____ Sold At $ _____

Location of Certificates _____ Comments _____

Broker _____ Telephone _____

Address _____ City _____ State _____

Account Is In The Name Of: _____ Account No. _____

Name of Commodity _____ Amount Purchased _____ Purchase Price $ _____

Transaction Date _____ Bought At $ _____ Sold At $ _____

Location of Certificates _____ Comments _____

Broker _____ Telephone _____

Address _____ City _____ State _____

Account Is In The Name Of: _____ Account No. _____

Name of Commodity _____ Amount Purchased _____ Purchase Price $ _____

Transaction Date _____ Bought At $ _____ Sold At $ _____

Location of Certificates _____ Comments _____

Mutual Funds

Mutual Fund Name _____   Account No. _____

Broker _____   Telephone No. _____

Address _____   City _____ State _____

Purchase Date _____ No. of Shares _____ Price Per Share _____

Comments: Location of contract, etc. _____

_____

_____

Mutual Fund Name _____   Account No. _____

Broker _____   Telephone No. _____

Address _____   City _____ State _____

Purchase Date _____ No. of Shares _____ Price Per Share _____

Comments: Location of contract, etc. _____

_____

_____

Mutual Fund Name _____   Account No. _____

Broker _____   Telephone No. _____

Address _____   City _____ State _____

Purchase Date _____ No. of Shares _____ Price Per Share _____

Comments: Location of contract, etc. _____

_____

_____

Mutual Fund Name _____   Account No. _____

Broker _____   Telephone No. _____

Address _____   City _____ State _____

Purchase Date _____ No. of Shares _____ Price Per Share _____

Comments: Location of contract, etc. _____

_____

_____

Other Investments

Date	Item	Description	Location

Savings Bonds

Date Purchased or Received	Serial Number	Cost	Maturity Value	Comments Date	Owner Beneficiary

Date Purchased or Received	Serial Number	Cost	Maturity Value	Comments Date	Owner Beneficiary

Personal Loans

Loaned to

Name_____ Date_____

Address_____ City_____ State_____

Type of Loan_____ Amount of Loan_____ Due Date_____ Interest_____

Comments_____

_____

_____

Loaned to

Name_____ Date_____

Address_____ City_____ State_____

Type of Loan_____ Amount of Loan_____ Due Date_____ Interest_____

Comments_____

_____

_____

Loaned to

Name_____ Date_____

Address_____ City_____ State_____

Type of Loan_____ Amount of Loan_____ Due Date_____ Interest_____

Comments_____

_____

_____

Loaned to

Name_____ Date_____

Address_____ City_____ State_____

Type of Loan_____ Amount of Loan_____ Due Date_____ Interest_____

Comments_____

_____

_____

*M*ost common Living Trusts are arrangements between a bank or trust company by which your present assets are legally entrusted to it for professional and skillful management while you are alive, and continued for a specific period after your death for the benefit of your heirs. Its main purpose is to establish a long period of financial security for yourself and your heirs.

There are basically two types of living trusts: a revocable trust, whereby you retain the right to amend or cancel at any time; and an irrevocable trust, whereby you give up your right to cancel for certain tax advantages. An irrevocable trust can be legally revoked only with the consent of all beneficiaries named in the trust.

A trust is as flexible as you need it to be. Just about anything of value can be placed in a trust: Life insurance, real estate, stocks, bonds, bank accounts, etc. There are a variety of trusts. Most Living Trusts allow you to be the trustee of your own assets during your lifetime.

All trusts have a termination date, which may vary from state to state. Setting up a trust is a very complicated matter, which should be accomplished with the aid of a lawyer who is familiar with the mechanics of local laws and their administration—as well as with the final disposition of your principal.

Following are some of the advantages:
a. Limit your estate to blood relatives. Protect children from a prior marriage.
b. You remain in control of all your assets in your lifetime by instructing your trustee as to how you wish your income and property handled after your death.
c. You can free yourself from financial management and the details of caring for securities and other properties.
d. A Living Trust is convenient for bridging financial transitions that occur at death or disability.
e. A Living Trust has tax savings advantages so that a larger estate can be left to your heirs.

f. If you travel, your property is continually and expertly managed.
g. You can prevent a child from blowing an inheritance.
h. In the event of death, your property continues to be managed professionally and is ultimately distributed to your heirs without delays, probate, or extra costs.
i. A Living Trust is strictly private unlike a will where everything you own, including your finances, is a matter of public record for everyone to see.
j. A Living Trust eliminates a lengthly and costly probate process. Your estate goes directly to your heirs.

A will does not protect your heirs against huge legal fees, executor or court fees. Probate sometimes takes months to settle and may cost as much as 10% of your estate before any heir receives a single dollar.

If it makes sense for you to have one, ask your attorney or banker how to draw up an agreement listing your instructions on how you wish your property to be protected and managed. Costs for Living Trust services are moderate and tax-deductible.

Living Trusts and Durable Power of Attorney should be reviewed and updated, as should your will, every five years or so. The documents themselves, if not given to the person designated to handle your financial affairs, should be filed with your personal papers. It may be a good idea to store a copy in your safe deposit box, making sure your designated agent or trustee has a power of attorney to open the box.

Testamentary trust is stated in your will and becomes active only after you die. The trustee is named in your will along with instructions on how your property is to be managed. This method is a safeguard against inexperience and relieves your heirs of the responsibilities which go with the management of securities and property.

Trust Fund Data

Type of Trust _____ Date Established _____

Established By _____

Trust Set Up By (Bank or Attorney): _____

Address _____ City _____ State _____

Beneficiary: Name _____

Address _____ City _____ State _____

Trust Agreement Located At: _____

Executor: _____

_____

Type of Trust _____ Date Established _____

Established By _____

Trust Set Up By (Bank or Attorney): _____

Address _____ City _____ State _____

Beneficiary: Name _____

Address _____ City _____ State _____

Trust Agreement Located At: _____

Executor: _____

_____

Type of Trust _____ Date Established _____

Established By _____

Trust Set Up By (Bank or Attorney): _____

Address _____ City _____ State _____

Beneficiary: Name _____

Address _____ City _____ State _____

Trust Agreement Located At: _____

Executor: _____

_____

Trust Fund Data

Type of Trust _____ Date Established _____

Established By _____

Trust Set Up By (Bank or Attorney): _____

Address _____ City _____ State _____

Beneficiary: Name _____

       Address _____ City _____ State _____

Trust Agreement Located At: _____

Executor: _____

_____

Type of Trust _____ Date Established _____

Established By _____

Trust Set Up By (Bank or Attorney): _____

Address _____ City _____ State _____

Beneficiary: Name _____

       Address _____ City _____ State _____

Trust Agreement Located At: _____

Executor: _____

_____

Type of Trust _____ Date Established _____

Established By _____

Trust Set Up By (Bank or Attorney): _____

Address _____ City _____ State _____

Beneficiary: Name _____

       Address _____ City _____ State _____

Trust Agreement Located At: _____

Executor: _____

_____

Personal Assets — Summary

	Value	Date		Value	Date		Value	Date
Cash In Checking								
Cash In Savings								
Life Insurance (Surrender Value)								
Stocks								
Bonds								
Commodities								
Real Estate (Market Value)								
Auto								
Annuities								
Cash Vested In Pension Plans								
Household Goods								
Antiques								
Jewelry								
Paintings								
Collections								
Business Interests								
Employer Benefits								
Other								
	Total			Total			Total	

Summary—Personal Assets

		Value	Date		Value	Date		Value	Date
Cash In Checking									
Cash In Savings									
Life Insurance (Surrender Value)									
Stocks									
Bonds									
Commodities									
Real Estate (Market Value)									
Auto									
Annuities									
Cash Vested In Pension Plans									
Household Goods									
Antiques									
Jewelry									
Paintings									
Collections									
Business Interests									
Employer Benefits									
Other									
		Total			Total			Total	

Liabilities—Fixed Bills

Taxes • Mortgage/Rent • Life Insurance • Utilities • Auto Insurance
Medical & Health Insurance • Installment Purchases • Student Loans
Personal Debts • Interest Due • Other Obligations

Due Date	Description	Amount	Date Paid	Annual Total		Total Owed

Fixed Bills — Liabilities

Taxes • Mortgage/Rent • Life Insurance • Utilities • Auto Insurance
Medical & Health Insurance • Installment Purchases • Student Loans
Personal Debts • Interest Due • Other Obligations

Due Date	Description	Amount	Date Paid	Annual Total		Total Owed

Liabilities—Fixed Bills

Taxes • Mortgage/Rent • Life Insurance • Utilities • Auto Insurance
Medical & Health Insurance • Installment Purchases • Student Loans
Personal Debts • Interest Due • Other Obligations

Due Date	Description	Amount	Date Paid	Annual Total		Total Owed

Fixed Bills – Liabilities

Taxes • Mortgage/Rent • Life Insurance • Utilities • Auto Insurance
Medical & Health Insurance • Installment Purchases • Student Loans
Personal Debts • Interest Due • Other Obligations

Due Date	Description	Amount	Date Paid	Annual Total		Total Owed

Property Taxes

Year	Description of Property	Taxed By	Amount	Date Paid	Date Paid

Year	Description of Property	Taxed By	Amount	Date Paid	Date Paid

Year	Description of Property	Taxed By	Amount	Date Paid	Date Paid

Property Taxes

Year	Description of Property	Taxed By	Amount	Date Paid	Date Paid

Year	Description of Property	Taxed By	Amount	Date Paid	Date Paid

Year	Description of Property	Taxed By	Amount	Date Paid	Date Paid

Major Financial Obligations

Year	Description	Amount	Date Paid

Income Tax Data

Year	Federal Tax Paid	State Tax Paid	Prepared By	Refund Received	Location of Records

Income Tax Data

Year	Federal Tax Paid	State Tax Paid	Prepared By	Refund Received	Location of Records

Income Tax Data

Year	Federal Tax Paid	State Tax Paid	Prepared By	Refund Received	Location of Records

Safe-Deposit Box Contents

Do's and Don'ts

Documents which are subject to theft or destruction by fire should be kept in a safe-deposit box. However, it is advisable to record all of the essential information in this book for quick reference. In the event of death, your safe-deposit box may be sealed by the bank until it can be examined by the IRS and state tax representatives. Cash, jewelry, bank books and other valuables found in a safe-deposit box can be considered as income to the decedent and liable to income and estate taxes.

Large amounts of cash and savings account passbooks should never be kept in a safe-deposit box. Your heirs will need this money to live on until insurance claims and death benefits are paid.

You should not keep a will or individual life insurance policy in a safe-deposit box. Immediate access to the will is essential in the event that it contains burial instructions or last wishes. Only a duplicate of a will should be kept in a safe-deposit box, with a note attached stating the location of the original.

Your life insurance policy should not be kept in a safe-deposit box; your family should have immediate access to file a claim. Upon death, a safe-deposit box can remain locked for many weeks or months.

Items that should be kept in a safe-deposit box:
Birth and marriage certificates
Deeds, mortgages, titles, agreements
Inventory of personal property
Citizenship papers
Military service records
Adoption papers

Divorce papers and other court decrees
Stock certificates
Marketable securities
Small family heirlooms
Passports
Stamp or coin collections

For married couples a joint safe-deposit box is advisable because it allows either party immediate access to important papers. In many states, however, a safe-deposit box that is held jointly is sealed when one of the owners dies, and can be opened only after obtaining an order from the probate court or the state tax authority. If you want access to a safe-deposit box solely owned by your spouse, your bank can give you a form that grants you access to the box, even though you are not a joint owner.

Others also may be granted access to your safe-deposit box, depending on bank policy. This usually requires a notarized statement authorizing access. Check with your bank to find out what constraints they offer precluding unauthorized safe-deposit box access.

Details of the contents of the safe-deposit box should be entered in this book and frequently updated to prevent future misunderstanding.

One of the best ways to safeguard important items and documents to which you need frequent access is in a locked, fire resistant box or safe kept at home.

Your family should know what to find in your safe deposit box when it is opened. Itemizing the contents here—and keeping the list current—will prevent misunderstanding and help your family quickly locate vital papers.

Contents — Safe Deposit Box

In The Name Of: _____

Bank _____

Address _____

Box Number _____

Location of Key _____

Authorized Signatures _____

_____

Names of Those Possessing Keys _____

_____

Contents: _____

_____

_____

_____

_____

_____

In The Name Of: _____

Bank _____

Address _____

Box Number _____

Location of Key _____

Authorized Signatures _____

_____

Names of Those Possessing Keys _____

_____

Contents: _____

_____

_____

_____

_____

_____

In The Name Of: _____

Bank _____

Address _____

Box Number _____

Location of Key _____

Authorized Signatures _____

_____

Names of Those Possessing Keys _____

_____

Contents: _____

_____

_____

_____

_____

_____

In The Name Of: _____

Bank _____

Address _____

Box Number _____

Location of Key _____

Authorized Signatures _____

_____

Names of Those Possessing Keys _____

_____

Contents: _____

_____

_____

_____

_____

_____

Personal Effects

Item Description	Date Acquired	Purchase Price	Location	Estimated Value

"*M*en fear death as children fear to go in the dark," wrote a famous poet. We are all reluctant to think about death, whether our own or that of loved ones. Yet our lives are marked by periodic encounters with death and we must prepare for the inevitable—and do so responsibly. The better prepared we are, the lighter will be the burden on those we love.

The passage of a person from life into death is signified by a funeral, one of the most ancient customs known to mankind. Different faiths and societies have evolved a variety of funeral services and rites, but all are conducted in a like spirit. They attest to the religious aspirations of the mourners and, at the same time, enable these family members and friends to pay final homage to the deceased. As much as a funeral denotes a death, it also commemorates life. We honor our dead by gathering together at a funeral to remember their lives, their personalities, and their achievements.

If you find yourself with the responsibility for arranging a funeral, you should be familiar with the basic principles described here. In this way you can offer effective help and support for the people you care about. And the time will come when your family must arrange your own funeral. You can make this task easier for them by setting down in these pages your recommendations and wishes.

Provide your family with the names and addresses of trusted friends or relatives whom they can call upon in time of need. In addition, make a list of the friends, associates, and organizations you would like notified. Compiling such a list without you will be an added trial for your family.

Many people purchase cemetery plots or burial vaults for themselves and other family members. If you have done so, enter all the relevant details, including the name of the person or organization to be contacted. File the deed with your vital papers. If you have not made burial plans as yet, it may be wise to consider doing so. Unless you request cremation, your family may be unable to purchase a suitable resting place at the moment when it is needed.

Any preferences, requests or special arrangements you would like carried out should also be written down and affirmed by your signature. These will serve as guidelines when your family has to decide upon a form or place of burial, or a particular type of service or monument. In making such decisions, the funeral director has an important role which many people overlook. His knowledge and experience are invaluable, for there is no standard form for a funeral. Along with your clergyman, if you have one, the funeral director can recommend and arrange the kind of service that will be most fitting for the deceased and that will suit the needs of the family. He will also fill out the death certificate and, if necessary, help prepare the obituary. Moreover, the funeral director can advise about the benefits to which the family may be entitled and assist with the paperwork involved. The Social Security program, for instance, provides benefits to certain survivors and dependents. Some fraternal organizations contribute to the funeral expenses of a deceased member. A family may also be eligible for burial allowances from the Veterans Administration. All the facts needed to file these claims—Social Security number, armed forces serial number, and so on—can be recorded in the appropriate places in this book. If you yourself have made provisions for your funeral expenses, describe the source of the funds here.

In The Event of Death

Location of Cemetery Deed _____

_____

Name of Cemetery _____

Address _____

_____

Trusted Friends to Be Contacted _____

_____

_____

_____

_____

_____

_____

_____

_____

_____

_____

_____

_____

_____

_____

Family Advisors _____

_____

_____

Organizations to Be Contacted _____

_____

_____

_____

_____

In The Event of Death

Funeral Preferences_____

_____

_____

_____

_____

Personal Requests_____

_____

_____

_____

_____

Have you expressed your right to
die with dignity?_____

_____

Comments:_____

_____

_____

_____

_____

_____

_____

_____

_____

_____

_____

Are you an organ donor?____ *(see next page)*

Which organs to which organizations?_____

_____

_____

_____

Special Arrangements_____

_____

_____

_____

_____

_____

_____

_____

Epitaph_____

_____

_____

_____

Monument_____

_____

_____

_____

_____

_____

Signature_____

Should You Be An Organ Donor?

How, When & Why

People of all races and religions—young and old alike—share in their ability to offer the gift of life. Surgical accomplishment has reached a level of sophistication making possible the transplant of virtually any organ, often several simultaneously.

The intent to exercise this ultimate act of compassion was expressed some time ago in the following way:

"The day will come when my body will lie upon a white sheet neatly tucked under four corners of a mattress in a hospital busily occupied with the living and the dying. At a certain moment a doctor will determine that my brain has ceased to function and that, for all practical purposes, my life has stopped.

"When that happens, do not attempt to instill artificial life into my body by the use of a machine. And don't call this my deathbed. Let it be called a "bed of life," and let my body be taken from it to help others lead fuller lives.

"Give my sight to the man who has never seen a sunrise, a baby's face, or love in the eyes of a woman. Give my heart to a person whose own heart has caused nothing but endless days of pain. Give my blood to a teenager who was pulled from the wreckage of his car, so that he might live to see his grandchildren play. Give my kidneys to one who depends on a machine to exist from week to week. Take my bones, every nerve and muscle in my body and find a way to make a crippled child walk.

"Explore every corner of my brain. Take my cells, if necessary, and let them grow so that, someday, a speechless boy will shout at the crack of a bat and a deaf girl will hear the sound of rain against her window.

"Burn what is left of me and scatter my ashes to the winds to help the flowers grow. If you must bury something, let it be my faults, my weaknesses, and all prejudice against my fellow man."*

This quotation is taken from "To Remember Me", by Robert N. Test.

As an organ donor you may choose to donate your heart, lungs, liver, kidneys, pancreas, corneas, bone, and tissue for transplantation. The transplantation team will evaluate the health of all the organs and their potential for transplantation at the time of death. Your wishes will be carefully followed.

Organ and tissue donation does not alter the appearance of the body or prevent or delay a scheduled funeral. Burial expenses remain the responsibility of the family or estate.

The best recipient will be chosen from patients awaiting a transplant. The choice is made by a transplant surgeon based on specific medical criteria. A number of factors usually are considered in the choice, such as blood type and length of time on the waiting list.

There is no charge for organ or tissue removal for transplantation. All costs associated with organ donation are paid by the organization that arranges for their transplantation.

Almost any person 18 years of age and older can become an organ donor. All that is necessary is to fill out and sign the Uniform Donor Card or the back of your driver's license. Two witnesses must also sign. If you are under 18 you may sign a donor card with the consent of your parent or guardian.

The decision to become an organ donor is an important one. Before you make it, talk it over with your family. It is essential that they understand your wishes, because after your death they are the only ones able to give final consent.

* Reprinted with permission, Ann Landers/Creators Syndicate

"To Soon Old and Too Late Smart."

Up to now the chapters in this book have dealt with tangible matters: vital statistics, medical history, insurance policies, possessions, business affairs and finances. But there is another, less obvious, area where you can give your family important information that will help them continue on without you.

Let your wishes be known about your hopes for the family's future—specific recommendations about the educational and career goals of your children; the ways in which you would like the family to uphold the tenets and obligations of your religious faith; or even ideas about ethical conduct in human relationships.

All these precepts and beliefs are in reality extensions of your personality and represent the knowledge you have acquired and the standards you have evolved during your lifetime. As such, these pages will constitute your personal legacy to your family. You may further want to recount your family's values, outstanding achievements, and laudable traits in the hope that future generations will follow the best precedents.

This is also the place to write down those old family sayings and proverbs which you have inherited and by which you would like your descendents to be guided.

In the course of your life you have naturally come by a great deal of knowledge and experience—a wealth of small but important things. Whether it's how to buy a car, where to take a vacation, or the best remedy for a cold, these ideas should be recorded for future reference; they could prove valuable to your family.

Equally valuable is the wisdom you have gained in each stage of life. Your observations on marriage, divorce, child rearing, retirement, death, or family relationships will be read with keen interest by others. They are your intangible assets, your personal philosophy, and thus as much a part of your estate, your family's inheritance from you, as real property.

There is no education like adversity.

Disraeli

Advice & Recommendations

Patience is a necessary ingredient of genius.
                                    Disraeli

_____ *Date* _____

_____

_____

_____

_____

_____

_____

_____

_____

_____

_____

_____

_____

_____

_____

_____

_____

_____

_____

_____

_____

_____

_____

_____

_____

Signature _____

Advice & Recommendations

The great pleasure in life is doing what people say you cannot do.

Walter Bagehot

_____ Date _____

_____

_____

_____

_____

_____

_____

_____

_____

_____

_____

_____

_____

_____

_____

_____

_____

_____

_____

_____

_____

_____

_____

_____

Signature _____

Glossary

Abandonment—a situation when one spouse leaves the other without an intention to return.

Abdication—a voluntary act where a person gives up a function or trust.

Abrogate—to revoke or cancel.

Abstract of Title—a short history of title to a piece of land, documented with facts, wills, grants, conveyances, and any other records.

Abut—to touch boundaries or to border on.

Abutting Owner—an owner of property that touches your border or is in close proximity to your property.

Access—legal right of a property owner whose land adjoins a road to use such a road to go to and from his property without road obstructions.

Accommodation—an agreement or arrangement whereby a loan is made by one person as a favor to another.

Adjuster—a person employed by an insurance company whose job is to investigate and settle claims for property damage or personal injury with the insured.

Administrator—one who is appointed to manage the estate of a person who has died and did not name an executor.

Adoption—voluntary act of accepting a child of other parents and giving the child all rights, privileges, and responsibilities as if it was your own. Adoption must be authorized by a state court.

Advancement—is an irrevocable gift of money or property made to an heir or used for the benefit of an heir with the anticipation that such property would have been inherited in a will.

Agent—one who is authorized to act for the benefit of another in business transactions or the management of property.

Agreement—is a meeting of the minds between two or more parties to conduct business or transfer from one to another rights, benefits or property.

Alimony—is a court order, a money allowance to one spouse from the other for support after a divorce or legal separation.

Amortization—payment of an indebtedness such as a mortgage by installments. A gradual extinguishment of a debt.

Annuity—is a fixed amount of money that is payable within a specific time frame or for life. It is generally granted, bequeathed, contracted, or purchased.

Annulment—an act to legally dissolve that which once existed, such as a marriage.

Appraisal—to set an estimated value on property by two or more qualified people in writing.

Arrears—overdue or unpaid debt or liability, although it is due to be paid.

Assessment—is evaluation of property to fix a value upon which a tax rate will be imposed.

Assets—anything of value and interest in real or personal property.

Assignment—an act whereby one transfers his rights and interests to another person.

Assured—is a person in whose name an insurance policy is issued. For instance: a mother insures her son's life for her benefit but the son has no interest in the property. You must have an insurable interest.

Attachment—a legal proceeding by which one's property is taken into legal custody to satisfy plaintiff's demand. Due process, a court hearing, is required before property is taken from an owner.

Attestation—the act of being a witness to the signing of a document. To affirm as true.

Bankruptcy—is a legal proceeding under the federal laws, dealing with the inability of a debtor to pay his debts as they become due.

Bearer—is the person who is holding a check, promissory note, a bill, or any negotiable instrument that is payable to him when presented for payment.

Beneficial Use — conveyed rights in respect to property and the right to enjoyment. Although the person does not own the property, the legal title is in one person's name or trust while the right to such use is in another name.

Beneficiary — is the one receiving, or perhaps designated to receive, the benefits or advantages stated in a will, trust, partnership, guardianship, or in an insurance policy.

Bequest — is a gift of personal property stated in a will.

Binder — a preliminary agreement for temporary insurance until a formal contract or policy is issued. Used in insurance and real estate.

Book Value — a net worth of a business or property as stated on the balance sheet.

Broker — is a person who brings two parties together such as a buyer or a seller and assists in negotiating contracts between them, whose compensation is a commission or a fee.

Capital — is a gross amount of money or property that is used or owned by an individual or corporation at a specific time.

Capital Gain — is a profit from the sale of certain property for more than its original cost.

Chattel Mortgage — is a document transferring legal interest by the owner of personal property and ownership to secure a repayment of a loan.

Check — is a negotiable instrument, ordering your bank, as a depositor, to pay a certain sum of monies to the order of the named receiver.

C.I.F. — is an abbreviation of "cost, insurance, and freight," an abbreviation mostly used in sales contracts to state the price of goods purchased, the cost of insurance, and freight charges.

Closing Of Title — is a time the buyer of real property pays the money due under the con-tract in exchange for the property deed.

Codicil — is a document that is executed with the same formality as a will to make changes in an existing will. It is a supplement to a will.

Co-Executor — is a person that is named in a will with one or more to perform certain responsibilities of an executor.

Coinsurance — a system of insurance whereby the insurer provides only a certain percentage of the insured's loss. The purpose is to reflect a relative division of risk between the insured and the insurer.

Collateral — to obtain credit it is often necessary to offer some personal and real property as security and place it within legal control of the lender. In the event of a default, the property can be sold and applied to the amount owing.

Common-Law Marriage — a relationship between a man and a women living together as husband and wife. Recognized by law as a valid marriage in many states.

Community Property — property that is acquired after marriage by both husband and wife and which is owned in common. Property that is acquired through a will, gift, or descent, or property that was owned by either spouse before the marriage is not considered community property.

Conditional Sale — is a written agreement which gives the buyer possession of property but not ownership until the property is paid for in full.

Conditional Will — is a will containing specified conditions and instructions how the property should be disposed only in the event of death.

Condominium — is an apartment building in which the apartment is owned by individuals and not by a corporation.

Contemplation of Death — is a situation when one is influenced by impending death to give

Glossary

away all or part of his property.

Contingent Fee—a fee that is paid to an attorney only when certain results are achieved.

Contract—is a written agreement between two or more people that is enforceable in a court of law.

Conveyance—a written instrument by which ownership of property or title is transferred from one person to another.

Cost, Insurance, and Freight (C.I.F.)—is a term used in a contract in the sale of merchandise which states that the seller will pay the insurance, cost, and freight of goods shipped to its point of destination.

Curtesy—is the husband's right to common-law property of his wife upon her death, provided they have had children capable of inheriting.

Creditor—a person to whom money is owed.

Custody—a legal right granted to a parent or another person to control, educate, and bring up a child, or care and keeping of property.

Debenture—a written document that acknowledges a debt.

Debt—money, services, or goods owed by one person to another.

Decedent—is a deceased person.

Deed—a real estate document in which ownership is transferred.

Dependent—a person who receives support from another.

Deposition—a written statement which is made under oath, outside the court for use as evidence in court.

Depreciation—a loss in value resulting from usage or deterioration.

Descent—a system of acquiring property from a decedent without a will.

Descendant—a person that is an offspring of another, or a remote offspring such as grandchildren or great-grandchildren.

Devise—is a document transferring real estate by a will.

Disinherit—is an act to prevent an heir from inheriting property that he normally would have inherited in the course of descent.

Dispossess—a court order issued at the request of the landlord to oust a tenant off his real estate.

Dissolution—means to terminate or cancel, such as a contract, a marriage by divorce, or the existence of a corporation.

Distributee—is a person who shares in the estate of someone who died without a will.

Dividend—a share of profits paid to stockholders or to policyholders in a mutual insurance society.

Divorce—a court order dissolving a marriage with the right to remarry.

Divorce Decree—a court document dissolving a marriage.

Domicile—a person's permanent address and home.

Dower—is the right of the widow to a share of the real estate her husband owned at the time of his death.

Easement—is the legal limited right of a landowner to use the land of his neighbor.

Endorsement—is a signature made on the back of a negotiable document by a person who owns it at the time when a transfer is made to someone else.

Endowment—in life insurance it provides payment of the face value of the policy during one's lifetime or on death while the policy is in effect.

Enoch Arden—is a legal proceeding which allows the dissolution of a marriage when one of the partners disappears for a designated period of time and creates a legal presumption that they are dead.

Estate—property belonging to a deceased

person which must be distributed or administered according to a will or by the intestacy laws.

Estate Tax—a tax levied on the privilege of transferring property by reason of death. This is not a property tax.

Eviction—a legal proceeding which orders a person or tenant to leave the premises or property.

Executor—a person appointed in a will to take charge of the estate and the administration according to terms stated in the will, subject to the supervision of the court.

Extended Coverage—is an insurance policy which covers damage resulting from a windstorm, hail, explosion, and other stated risks.

Extortion—an unlawful manner of taking money or property from a person by threat or duress or by abuse of authority.

Face Amount—the actual amount indicated in writing without taking into consideration interest, dividends, or any other factors that would change the sum.

Factor—a commission merchant who takes the property or merchandise of another to sell for himself. Sometimes it's a company who takes over the accounts receivable of a business to collect the monies due for a large commission.

Fair Market Value—is a price a willing buyer would pay and the seller would accept under normal circumstances.

Fee Simple—designates absolute ownership. The owner has absolute right to dispose of his property during his lifetime or pass his absolute rights to whomever he wishes when he dies.

Fiduciary—Person who has a special relation in trust, confidence and duty to act for the benefit of another person.

F.O.B.—an abbreviation for "freight on board."

Means the buyer will pay the expense of shipping and insurance of goods to their destination from a designated origin.

Foreclosure—is a legal court proceeding by which real estate or personal property is taken and sold to satisfy a mortgage debt.

Forfeit—means to lose or surrender rights, property, or privileges as a result of omission, offense, error, crime, misconduct, or breach of contract.

Gift—is a voluntary act in transfer of property.

Gift Tax—is a tax levied by the federal government on gifts of money or property.

Grant—is a document by which real property or an interest in real property is transferred.

Gross Estate—means total value of all property that is left by a deceased person.

Gross Income—total income from all sources of a taxpayer before any taxes, deductions, and exemptions are made.

Group Insurance—a system of life, accident, or health insurance covering members of a group under a single contract.

Guardian—a person who is appointed to care for another person or property who is not competent to act in his own best interest, such as an infant or a minor.

Heir—a person who inherits either real estate or personal property either by will or intestate when someone dies without a will.

Holder—is a person who is in legal possession of a check, bill of exchange, a promissory note, or any document of title and who is entitled to receive payment.

Holding Company—a supercorporation which is organized to hold and control stock in one or more other corporations.

Holographic Will—is one that is written in the handwriting and signed by the maker or testator.

Homestead—property that is exempt from sale

Glossary

or attachment by a creditor to pay for homeowner's general debts.

Hypothecate — is to pledge property for security without a formal transfer of possession.

Illegitimate Child — a child that is born to unmarried parents.

Indemnity — in insurance, is the reimbursement for losses sustained.

Infant — a person who has not attained the legal age, generally 21. Also known as a minor.

Inheritance — refers only to real or personal property that is passed down by descent.

Inheritance Tax — a tax that is levied on the passing of property by descent or will. It is not a tax on the property itself.

Instrument — a written legal document such as a contract, a will, a lease, or a check.

Insolvent — a financial condition of an individual, a business, or corporation when the liabilities are greater than the assets and debts cannot be paid as they fall due.

Insurable Interest — is either ownership or interest a person must have to be able to take out an insurance policy to protect that interest.

Interest — is the charge made for the use of money, such as for a loan. It can also be a share in the ownership of property, commercial enterprise, or a financial undertaking.

Inter Vivos — Latin for "between the living." Transactions made by one living person for the benefit of another while that person is living.

Intestacy — is when a person dies without leaving a valid will.

Invalid — not legally binding. Having no authority.

Issue — a direct descendant, such as a child, grandchild, and so forth.

Jointly Owned Property — property that is owned by two or more individuals, regardless of their relationship.

Joint Will — a will drawn up and signed by more than one person with the intention that the same will is of each of them.

Kin — those who are related by blood.

Landlord — one who leases real property for an agreed period of time at a specific rent.

Lapse — termination of a right or privilege due to failure to perform a certain act.

Lease — a written contract that grants the exclusive use of property for a specific period at an agreed rent.

Legacy — also known as a bequest. A gift of certain personal property to a named individual in a will.

Letters of Administration — are court documents issued by either a probate or surrogate court which give a named administrator the authority to administer the estate of a person who died without leaving a will.

Letters Testamentary — are court documents issued either by a probate or surrogate court giving the executor, who is named in the will, the authority to administer the estate of the deceased.

Liability — being responsible for damages which result from either intentional or negligent acts. A duty which must be performed.

Liable — accountable or responsible for.

License — a document which grants permission to do something which could not be done legally without such permission.

Lien — is a legal claim against the property of another as security for some debt or charge.

Life Estate — is an estate held by a tenant throughout his lifetime.

Life Insurance Trust — is an agreement between the insured person and his trustee which instructs the trustee how the insurance policy proceeds are to be managed or distributed to the beneficiaries upon his death.

Life Interest — is an interest which lasts only for

the duration of the life of the person to whom the interest is given.

Liquid Assets — all property that can be quickly converted into cash.

Liquidated — means settled, determined the amount due, and paid the amount. Satisfying the indebtedness.

Living Trust — is a trust that is created during one's lifetime. A testamentary trust is created by a will after death.

Malpractice — improper, negligent, or unethical conduct by a doctor, lawyer, or someone holding an official or professional position.

Marital Deduction — under the Federal Estate and Gift Tax Statute, it permits a spouse to take, tax free, up to half of the value of the decedent's adjusted gross estate.

Mechanic's Lien — attaches the land and the buildings for the purpose of securing a priority payment for work and materials that were supplied by an artisan or construction company in the construction or repair of a building.

Mediator — a person who serves as a go-between for two parties in an effort to reconcile differences.

Merger — is the absorption of all corporate assets of one corporation by another; therefore, the individual existence is discontinued.

Minor — a person under legal age, usually twenty-one years of age.

Misrepresentation — any representation by a statement, conduct, contract, or any other document which is misleading, incorrect, or dishonest.

Monopoly — is the exclusive control of an article of trade or service that is controlled by an individual or one group by means of production and distribution.

Mortgage — is a contract which pledges your property to a creditor, for a specific time, as security for the repayment of a loan.

Multiple Wills — are photocopies of the same will; each is executed as if it were an original.

Mutual and Reciprocal Wills — are separate wills, executed by individual persons, which contain interchangeable provisions for the distribution and disposition of their personal property in line with agreements between them.

Necessaries — are basic essentials which every person needs for sustenance and reasonable enjoyment of life, such as food, shelter, clothing, and education.

Negligence — is the failure of a person to use care and reasonable judgment, which he is obligated to use by law, to protect the rights and property of others in a particular set of circumstances.

Negotiable Instrument — is a document such as a check, note, or a bill of exchange which, when executed, transfers legal ownership to another person which enables him to demand the full amount stated on the face of the instrument.

Negotiate — to discuss and arrange an agreement of sale or a contract, or to transfer a document, a negotiable instrument, from one owner to another by endorsement.

Net — is the portion that remains after all deductions, expenses, or losses.

Next of Kin — a person or persons most closely related to the decedent by blood.

Nominal — something that exists in name only, without legal share or interest.

Nonage — not within a legal age to do something.

Non Compos Mentis — a general phrase which applies to all phases of mental incapacity.

Note — is a negotiable instrument, a signed promise by one person to pay another a certain sum of monies at a specified time.

Glossary

Notice—actual communication of information by an authorized person to an individual.

Novation—results when a new obligation is made for an old one. An agreement whereby one debt is substituted for another or one creditor for another.

Nuisance—a source of inconvenience and annoyance.

Null—having no legal force or validity.

Nuncupative Will—is an oral will made before witnesses in situations of extreme illness in the anticipation of dying. Many states do not honor a nuncupative will. Some states only honor it in specific situations.

Occupancy—is taking possession of real property without legal ownership.

Open Shop—an establishment that employs both union and nonunion workers.

Option—is a right or privilege of either buying or selling something within a specified time at a specified price.

Oral—spoken, not written words.

Orphan—generally a minor or an infant who has lost both or sometimes one parent.

Owner—is the person who has a legal right and title to property.

Ownership—is a person's exclusive right of possessing, enjoying, and disposing of his property.

Palimony—financial separation settlement between two unmarried people who have lived together.

Paramount Title—a title which will prevail over another. It generally signifies an immediate right of possession.

Partition—is the dividing of property into separate parcels so that each parcel may be owned individually.

Partnership—a relationship that is formed by contract between two or more competent persons to combine their money, labor, and skill in business and to divide the profits and bear the loss in certain proportions.

Par Value—face value that is imprinted on a stock certificate or bond which provides the basis on which interest or dividends are paid.

Passport—an official document issued by a government to a person certifying his identity and citizenship and requesting foreign governments to grant safe passage and all legal protection while within their jurisdiction.

Patent—a government grant to an inventor, assuring him the exclusive right to make, use, or sell his invention for a certain period of time.

Per Capita—Latin phrase meaning "per person"; according to the number of individuals who share and share alike. When anything is figured per capita the total is equally divided among all the individuals.

Perpetuities, Rule Against—a rule whereby the full ownership of a piece of property cannot be delayed more than a lifetime plus twenty-one years.

Per Stirpes—Latin phrase meaning "through or by roots or stock, by representation." It's the distribution of an estate of the deceased with reference of descent. It gives the descendants each a share in the estate, not equal but a proper share to which the person is entitled in relationship to the ancestor.

Pledge—is the use of personal property as security for the payment of a loan or other obligation.

Possession—a control over property; the having, holding, or detention of property in one's power or command, with or without rightful ownership.

Postdated Check—is one that is complete in all respects but dated in the future and is only payable on or after the date stated on the check.

Posthumous Child—a child who is born after the death of its father.

Post Mortem—Latin phrase for "after death." This phrase generally refers to the examination of the body of the deceased to determine the cause of death.

Power of Appointment—a power and authority given by one person to another, in a will or deed, to dispose this property or interest to persons stated in his will.

Power of Attorney—a legal document by which one person grants the authority to another to perform certain specified acts on his behalf.

Preemption—a privilege granted by law to a settler upon public land to purchase the property on which he is settled at a specified price over the preference of other applicants.

Prenuptial Agreement—document prepared prior to marriage which states how property is to be divided in the event of divorce, separation or death of either spouse.

Premium—monies paid by the insured to an insurance company. In return the insurance company agrees to pay for damages or loss agreed on in the policy.

Prescription—is a legal method of acquiring an easement or interest in the land of another by continued regular use for a period set by statute.

Primogeniture—a law of descent whereby the eldest son of the same parents takes all the property or title of the decent father, excluding all other children of the same parent.

Principal—capital, or property, or financial holdings, as distinguished from the interest or revenue from it. A sum of money owed on a debt, upon which interest is calculated.

Privacy—the right of an individual or business to be left alone from public participation or publicity.

Privilege—a specific benefit, advantage, or favor granted to an individual under special conditions.

Privity—a relationship that is private or secret between individuals. A relationship between individuals sufficiently close to support a legal claim on behalf of or against another person with whom this relation exists.

Probate of a Will—is a court procedure which determines the validity of a will of the decedent. Legal establishment of the validity of the will before the disposition of the estate is made according to its provisions.

Proceeds—amount of money derived from the sale of property or a fund-raising venture.

Process—a summons or writ ordering the defendant to appear in court.

Promissory Note—is a written document, a promise by one person to pay to another person named in the document a certain sum of money at a specified time or on demand.

Property—tangible or intangible things to which its owner has unrestricted legal right to enjoy and dispose of.

Proprietory—exclusively belonging to or owned by an individual.

Proprietor—an individual who has an exclusive right or title to something

Pro-Rata—something that is distributed by a proportion or percentage.

Protective Order—a court order forbidding one person to continue to harass or threaten to harm another. Also, a court order against the normal legal system that might cause an injustice.

Proxy—a person who is given the authority by another to represent him or act or vote for him at stockholders or annual corporate meetings.

Purchase Money Mortgage—a mortgage given by the buyer to the seller to secure a part or all of the selling price at the time of purchase.

Glossary

Putative Father—a father of an illegitimate child.

Rape—crime of forcing a person to have intercourse against his or her will.

Real Estate—is land, also an interest in land and any structure or article that is attached to the land.

Receiver—is a person appointed by the court to take into his control and management property and funds to be disposed of at a later date by order of the court.

Recover—is the restoration of a person's property and rights, usually effected by legal proceedings.

Redemption—is an act of recovering property that may have been pledged or mortgaged.

Register—is a formal or official recording of names, actions, or items.

Reinsurance—is to acquire new insurance by the insurer from another insurance company against risks that were previously assumed.

Relation—a person who is related by blood or marriage.

Release—to relieve another person from debt or obligation. A document which transfers one person's right in property to another who is in actual possession.

Remainder—the part of an estate that is left after all the provisions in a will have been fulfilled.

Rent—monies paid to another person for the use, possession, and enjoyment of his property for specific periods stated in a lease.

Replevin—a legal process to regain personal property which was unlawfully taken or held.

Residuary Clause—is a clause in a will which transfers to the beneficiary portions of his property that the testator did not dispose of in his will.

Revocation of a Will—is an act by a person who has made a will that he is canceling or terminating his intentions and that his will shall no longer be effective.

Risk—is a danger or probability of loss. In insurance, specific events are covered by a policy, and the amount the insurance company stands to pay in the event damage or loss does occur.

Robbery—a forcible felonious act of taking property from a person against his will under fear or force.

Satisfaction Piece—is a document stating that a recorded mortgage or debt or other obligation has been satisfied.

Secured Creditor—is a creditor who holds the mortgage or a lien on property as security for payment of debt.

Security—something that is deposited, given, or pledged, which assures the fulfillment of an obligation or debt.

Securities—are stock certificates, bonds, or other negotiable instruments which convey indebtedness or a right created to participate in profits or assets in a profit-making enterprise. A written assurance for return of payment.

Seizure—a legal act taking real estate or personal property into possession.

Separation—is determined by a court which grants a husband and wife the right to live apart, although most of their marital obligations continue.

Separation Agreement—a document where husband and wife have agreed to stop living together. This document also provides support for the wife and children as well as the distribution of their property.

Sequestration—is a legal proceeding whereby property belonging to a debtor, or to a husband who failed to pay alimony, is taken and sold to satisfy his obligation. Holding property until indebtedness has been paid.

Solvency—is a position of having the ability to pay all debts or legal claims to one's creditors.

Spendthrift Trust—a trust whereby the trustee

is given the authority to distribute only the profits to the beneficiary. The principal remains out of reach of creditors. Such a trust is created to provide a fund for an incapable person only for his lifetime.

Stock Certificate—is a written instrument stating a share in the ownership of a corporation.

Sublease—is a transaction whereby a tenant grants an interest to another tenant but retains his interest for the term of the original lease.

Succession—is the sequence in which one person after another acquires a title or an estate.

Summons—court order that notifies a person that a lawsuit has been started against him and that he must appear in court to defend the charges against him or risk a court judgement against him by default.

Surety—a pledge or a formal promise by one person to guarantee payment or obligation of another.

Surrogate—a judge or a judicial officer who has the authority to probate wills and administer estates and guardianships.

Tenancy—is the possession or occupancy of land or a building by title, under a lease, or on payment of rent.

Tenant—is one who temporarily occupies a building or land which is owned by another, generally under terms stated in a lease.

Tender—a formal offer of money or service in payment of an obligation.

Tenure—a permanence of position or title granted to an employee after a specific number of years of employment.

Term—is a specific period of time. A point of time beginning or ending a period.

Testamentation—is a right and a privilege given to a person to find ways of disposing of his property by will.

Testament—a written document for instructing the disposition of one's personal property after death. Also better known as a will.

Testator—is a person who has made a legal will disposing of all his property before death.

Title—legal evidence, a document that constitutes the fullest right to own, control, and dispose of property.

Tort—a wrongful act which results in damage or injury done willfully, through negligence, or in circumstances involving liability but not involving breach of contract where a civil suit can be brought.

Trademark—an officially registered name, logo, or mark, affixed by a manufacturer to his goods to identify and distinguish them from competing goods.

Transfer—is an act whereby a title or interest in personal or real estate property is transferred to another person.

Trespass—is the act of entering the property of another without permission, either intentionally or unintentionally.

Trust—is a legal title to property held by one party, called the trustee, for the benefit of another, who is the beneficiary. Trust is the confidence given to another person, a trustee, who has legal title to property to administer for another person according to stated provisions of the creator of the trust.

Trustee—is a person, an agent, a bank, or a trust company holding legal title to property for a person to administer it for a beneficiary. The trustee is required to carry out specific duties with regard to property administration and disposition for another's benefit.

Trust Fund—is either real estate or personal property held in trust by a trustee for the benefit of another person.

Underwrite—to insure the satisfaction of an obligation or to assume the risk by way of insurance. To underwrite a stock or bond issue is to insure the sale of stock or bonds by agreeing to buy back all certificates at face value if they are not sold by a specified date.

Use — the right of a beneficiary to the employment of profits of land and buildings whereby the legal title and possession are vested in another who holds them in trust.

Usury — is an interest rate or demand for a loan of money which is in excess of the rate authorized within the state law.

Vendor — is a person who sells something.

Vest — is to give legal ownership of property or a right of present or future enjoyment.

Vested Interest — is a fixed, immediate right to the present and future enjoyment of certain rights and property. You have the right to sell or dispose of your vested interests to another individual.

Vested Right — is a fixed, immediate right to present and future enjoyment, sometimes by tenure, which is not subjected to any contigency.

Voidable — a condition of being made void but not necessarily void.

Voting Trust — is whereby a trust is created

by shareholders and their stock is deposited with a trustee or trustees. The shareholders retain ownership of their stock, but voting powers are delegated to the trustee or trustees.

Waiver — is a written instrument by which one relinquishes his rights, advantage, claim, or privilege.

Warranty — an assurance by the seller of property that the goods or the property are as presented or will be as promised in writing.

Whole Life Insurance — a policy that is in force as long as premiums are paid. The policy payment remains the same. The cash value remains the same. The policy accumulates dividends while it's in effect.

Will — a written legal declaration of how a person intends to dispose of his estate after his death. A deliberate decision, conclusion, or intention by a person who is of authority and power to arrive at his own decision.

Without Recourse — is an endorsement and passing of a negotiable instrument whereby the endorser accepts no liabilities for its payment.

NOTE

For more up-to-date information on legal matters that are pertinent to your need, visit your local library or book store. By being informed you can save thousands of dollars in fees and avoid costly mistakes. For your own peace of mind it is always best to know all your options before making an important decision.

Recording Information, Mounting Photographs, Adding Storage Envelopes

<u>What Every Family Should Know</u> has been designed as an easy permanent organizer for vital family records. It provides a place for everything so that everything is in one place. The following suggestions and recommendations are intended to help you achieve good results.

Before making a permanent entry, double-check all information for correct dates, places, names and spelling. Remember that family members will use this as a reference book. All information and entries should be recorded in ink. For best results use a dark ink, (blue-black or black) ball point or a fine felt tip pen. We recommend that you fill in each part slowly and accurately. Keep this book in a safe but an accessible place.

MOUNTING PHOTOGRAPHS—When mounting photographs apply adhesive sparingly to each back corner of the photograph. Press the photograph down firmly and rub each corner to smooth out the adhesive. Before closing the book, remove any excess adhesive that may have seeped out from under the photograph. To assure that the pages do not stick together, you may want to place a sheet of waxed paper or cellophane between the pages while the adhesive is drying.

As a precaution we do not recommend using liquid glues that spill easily or that tend to run between pieces of paper when squeezed together. Adhesives such as household cement or a glue stick will work very well. (Do not use water-based adhesive; they may shrink and warp the page when dry). Regardless of what you choose, use any adhesive sparingly and be certain to follow manufacturer's directions for cementing paper and photographs.

The picture areas throughout this book are all the same, 3" × 3¾". If a photo is too large for the designated space, you may trim the background and highlight only the subject. When trimming a photo, be certain to carefully measure and mark the photo before you cut. You may wish to use a metal ruler and an X-ACTO knife for greater accuracy.

If your photo is too large or too small, you can take it to your local photo dealer and explain your needs to him. He can make a print of only the area you want and to the size you need.

BOOK PRODUCTION CHARACTERISTICS— The binding in this book is Smyth sewn; the book cover hinges are reinforced —made to expand as documents and additional pages are added. Please use common sense as to how many documents you add between the covers of this book. The paper is acid free; it will not turn yellow, under normal conditions, and it will not turn brittle. We will replace this book without cost to you should a manufacturing defect develop. We welcome all suggestions in how we can improve this book.